7

ESSENTIALS
OF KIDS PRAYER **2.0**

Reflecting God's Glory

Angie Clark

All Scriptures are quoted from the
New Living Translation unless otherwise noted.

ACKNOWLEDGEMENTS

Without the direction of the Holy Spirit, I could have been lost at any point in this journey. Thank you, God, for keeping me close and lighting the way.

To my parents, your example and heritage have led me down paths of righteousness, over dirt roads of grace, and safely through traffic jams of doubt. "Sank you".

To every mentor and nurturer who claims me as your own, thank you for speaking into my life. I choose to believe all the nice things you say about me will be true...some day.

Special thanks to my unofficial 7 Essentials team of readers, proofers, and idea tweekers. You've helped me make something old new again. We ought to do this again some time.

And last but not least, thanks to all who read this and share my belief that children are an integral part of the Body of Christ, and that our purpose in life is to bring God glory. Without each other our lives wouldn't reflect nearly as much of Him as we'd like.

PART ONE

HANDBOOK CONTENT

PART TWO

BONUS MATERIAL

Foreword

By Thetus Tenney

"But Samuel ministered before the Lord, being a child..."
(1 Samuel 2:18).

Could it have been said more beautifully or with any more clarity? The child, ministering.

If ever there were doubts concerning the ability of children to hear the voice of the Lord or to minister before the Lord, the classical Biblical story of young Samuel is confirmation of the fact that God speaks to and ministers through children. The story of young Samuel continues, *"And the child Samuel ministered unto the Lord before Eli"*. The wise old priest, Eli, recognized the hand of the Lord on the child. He instructed and trained him in the ways of the Lord, in hearing the voice of the Lord and responding accordingly. As a result of this wise understanding, acceptance, and training of the young Samuel the Word of the Lord came to all Israel (2 Samuel 4:1).

In this book you will be challenged to re-discover how God has and does work through children.

~A word from the Lord came to the young girl who was one of Naaman's maids and a major miracle resulted.

~A prophetic dream came to young Joseph that ultimately had eternal impact.

~The endless kingdom of David had its beginning when he was a young man, just a 'stripling' (I Samuel 17).

My love for prayer started somewhere around the age of four, when I would accompany my oldest sister to her prayer time. My

9

earliest memory of being impacted by the Scriptures was at my mother's knee long before I could ever read for myself. I vividly recall experiencing the reverential fear of the Lord as I personally observed miracles, signs, and wonders in my early years. These are priceless treasures in my bank of memories and experiences. God knows, watches and calls children from their mother's wombs (Isaiah 44:24; Jeremiah 1:5).

We sometimes forget how many of the sacred stories that have inspired our faith involved the young. The stories of the young man, the son of a widow, and young Jairus' daughter who were both raised from the dead and the story of the boy with the lunch that fed the multitude, are just three of such accounts. The early church was blessed by the ministry of the young evangelist, Timothy, who was trained in the ways of the Lord as a child.

In this book, Angie, has not 'discovered' anything new. Rather, she is helping us all 're-discover' this unique part of God's story through the ages.

The involvement, training, and ministry of children in the ways of the Lord have been a part of all historic revivals. This is also a biblical precedent. It was eight-year-old Josiah who led Israel in the re-discovery of the ways of the Lord, which resulted in great revival. As a mother, grandmother, and a great-grandmother I rejoice in anticipation!

Read this book with open mind and heart. Three times it is recorded Jesus said "allow the little children to come." These are the words of the Mighty One who came as a baby and lived as a child. He still welcomes children.

Part One Introduction: FIRST, DELIGHT

An odd thing happened one Sunday morning during my first grade class prayer time. Immediately after taking prayer requests for boo-boos and scrapes, I was taken aback when the recently promoted students got up in unison and turned around to kneel at their seats. They proceeded to bury their heads in their arms and peeked at each other as I prayed. They were waiting for me to say the final, "Amen!"

Breaking that habit proved harder than I thought it would be because I had to go searching for the answer. Furthermore, I didn't have a clue where to begin. But I knew one thing. The answer wasn't trading their old class' habit for my new ones. They deserved more.

That Sunday marked the beginning of a quest to find the answer about what was missing and how to nurture it into existence. Now, years later, I think I can put my finger on it. They were lacking in delight. I couldn't see it then because so was I. At the time I thought delight was a word spoken mostly by spiritual kooks or old timers. I did okay with the idea of discipline, but had difficulty fathoming the concept of delighting in God. These days, I'm getting better at it, but it has been quite a process.

The Chicken Or The Egg

I understand now that discipline comes after delight, not the other way around. Let me explain it this way. For some of you, you delight in working out and staying fit, so you are disciplined about what you eat and how you take care of yourself. For others, like me, we have tried to discipline ourselves to work out and stay fit.

We can keep it up for a while, but then, at some point because we don't delight in it, or perhaps we delight more in something else, we lose our grip on discipline.

In a discipline-first paradigm, something has to change to bring about a delight-first ignition. Discipline in and of itself kills. This reminds me of something Paul wrote to the Corinthians. In his case, he explained the law was given to point out mistakes not to bring life. Focusing on following rules to reach a spiritual goal just makes us humans prideful or good at getting around them. Discipline for discipline's sake saps us, much like the letter of the law brought death in the Old Testament.

> *He has enabled us to be ministers of his new covenant. This is a covenant not of written laws, but of the Spirit. The old written covenant ends in death; but under the new covenant, the Spirit gives life* (2 Corinthians 3:6).

If a person's motivation for prayer is part of keeping a set of rules, then they are pretty much on their own. If someone prays every day just to follow the rules to avoid going to hell well, they would have just illustrated my point. On the other hand, if a person's motivation is to grow a relationship with God, or to do something he enjoys, then the odds of developing delight and unintended discipline just went through the roof. It's a choice.

Likability Factor

As you approach building a delight-first ignition switch, it may help to understand this is a very literal thing. The likability factor of any spiritual growth endeavor does matter. You gotta like it if you're gonna do it long-term. As an example, if you like shopping, you go shopping and are an amazingly good excuse-finder for going shopping. If you don't like shopping, you put it off, rush through it, or make an attempt occasionally when someone drags you out by your ear.

If you don't like a spiritual endeavor, ask yourself why, so you can build in some delight. If your kids don't like prayer, ask them why so you can discover ways to help make prayer enjoyable or, as kids would say it, "fun." Find ways, plural, to pump up the likability quotient for success.

What does delight feel like to you? It's taken me a while to learn to feel it and express it for myself. For me, delight is that slightly light-hearted feeling I get when I really like something or someone; I don't feel threatened but do feel comfortable. It also leaves an aftertaste of being satisfied. I challenge you to take a moment to write down what delight feels like to you. It's probably not going to be as easy as it would seem.

You see? It's not rocket science or spiritual hocus pocus, rather something a little more down to earth. Knowing this just may give you the edge to lead children who *want* to pray. Initially getting kids to *want* to pray springs from likability.

Since we're here, have you ever heard of a Tiger-Mom? Did you just cringe? In short, it's a kind of person who puts discipline above everything and everyone else. I'm so glad Jesus isn't a "Tiger-Mom" kind of guy. He puts a high value on delight rather than discipline as a motivator. He delights in me, period. He delights in you too. Period. He even delights in that kid who pushes your buttons during class. Accepting His delight in me is a key step in experiencing His glory, which ignites my delight for Him.

Delight

Experiencing His Glory

Back to that odd Sunday morning prayer time. As I hacked my way through a jungle of books, studies, seminars, and even some prayer coaching, I discovered something important. I felt most delighted in prayer after experiencing something connected to God's glory. In hindsight, this is what I started noticing in class with my kids, but only recently know how to put it into words.

When we shared present day stories of God's miracles, provision or care with our kids, they lit up during prayer. When we put prayer after an experience like this, there was a sense of delight in the discipline of prayer. No more turning around and burying their heads. No sir-ee. Kids, even shy ones, were volunteering to pray empathetically for others they knew or heard about.

How about you? When do you feel most energized, delighted, or plugged in for prayer?

Looking For God's Glory

Listening to Kevin Wheeler speak about his experiences while carrying a cross on wheels around the world was spellbinding. Kevin is not your average missionary. He carries a large wooden cross—on wheels—wherever he feels God leads him to go. If you can name it, he's probably got a story for it: Iraq, China, Tibet, Muslim nations, the Americas, Europe, Africa, and Asia.

At the start of his session, he gave a brief devotional that changed how I think about God's glory. According to Isaiah 6:3, God's glory fills all the earth. According to Kevin, it is our delight to find it, point it out, and reflect it. Last I heard, Kevin is still popping wheelies somewhere in the world, so I know God's glory is still being discovered in some corner of the earth, perhaps even for the first time. If you want to know more of Kevin's story, go to www.kw.org.

Thanks to my mom, I am a missions junkie. I love the old stories and really like to hear the emerging ones like Kevin's. If you are looking for information that exposes God's glory in the earth, missions stories from any age is a great place to start. As His glory impacts you, you'll find yourself looking for it in present day, in your very own personal space.

It's All About Him

In certain circles, referring to God's glory usually evokes images of a "glory cloud" or perhaps gold dust settling on people who are praying, or a service without preaching. Imagine that. But that's not exactly the glory Isaiah refers to, nor I, for that matter.

I'm referring to the glory God gets just from being Himself which has nothing to do with you or me. How refreshing. With God, it's supposed to be all about Him. And it's not just a catchy slogan. Now that's what I call awesome. He doesn't need me. He wants me. What person wouldn't melt believing that? And even in that melting, the glory would be His.

Too often we are unfazed by the simple things that evoke His glory because we make life all about us. Shifting our focus back to Him will enable us to see the glory He receives when someone turns to Him first instead of to a best friend. Or, the glory He gets when a person refuses to gripe or gossip, which also robs the enemy of any glory. If it's all about Him, you'll even be able to see a glimmer of His glory in a repeat-after-me prayer mumbled by someone struggling with low self-esteem. Look around. The earth is full of His glory. It really is all about Him.

Spiraling Upward

I see a bit of a pattern here. God's glory fuels my delight. Delight fuels my discipline. Discipline enriches my life. My enriched life deepens my relationship with God. My relationship allows me to get close enough to reflect His glory, which in turn fuels my delight. And the spiral keeps on spiraling, each pass widening my understanding and expanding my delight, onward and upward.

As you begin or extend your journey into the 7 Essentials of Kids Prayer, my hope is for you to be moved often by the Holy Spirit. I am praying He gives you insight about building that delight-first ignition switch for your kids so Jesus can truly be the center of their universe. After all, it's all about Him.

May you inspire delight in prayer, and reflect much glory.

PART ONE

HANDBOOK

Chapter 1: LISTENING
Hearing And Obeying God's Voice

CORE VALUE – John 10:27
My sheep recognize my voice; I know them, and they follow me.

Most of the time when we invite children to pray, especially in a corporate setting, it's to ask God for something. Seldom do we give children a chance to corporately or individually take time to listen for God to speak to them. Perhaps it's because we use a closely scripted curriculum and don't have time to train, only time to teach. Perhaps we have reservations about the very idea of anyone hearing God's voice, let alone children.

Whatever the reason, I am concerned that holding back from training in this area is playing right into the hands of the enemy. If he can keep us from listening for and hearing God speak directly, he has unfettered influence on our perceptions, especially in these last days.

I'm guessing most anyone reading this material believes that we are living in what is described as the end time. To borrow a great quote from renowned prophecy teacher Irvin Baxter, I'm not referring to the end of time, rather, "the end of human government and the transition to the kingdom of God." Without going into detail, suffice it to say that this transition period is going to be horrific for the world, tough on the Church, and full of spiritual turbulence. We need as many spiritual ears as possible, trained to clearly hear what the Spirit is saying in these times.

In the previous release of the 7 Essentials material, the goal was to get children activated in the Body of Christ. In this release, the goal is to corporately reflect God's glory back to Him, making all our efforts about Him.

To know how to bring Him glory means being able to hear His voice. Teachers, even preachers don't have all the answers all the time. I'm not suggesting that we shouldn't get guidance from mentors and elders in our lives, but I am suggesting that we will live more fulfilled lives as we acquire the spiritual muscle-memory of turning to God first.

Learning to discern God's voice, trusting Him, and proving Him are the things that will sustain us in difficult times. Walking in alignment is the essential element upon which all others hinge. When a person hears God, obeys Him and proves or trusts Him, it's that much harder for the enemy's fiery darts to hit their mark. I didn't realize this in 2006, when the first edition of this book rolled off the printer in our little office, but I see it now and thought it would be in all of our best interests if I didn't keep it to myself. Time will tell.

If you're new to this concept, I invite you to study the Word and visit places that have experience in this area. Check out pages 141-158 for more information. Many times, seeing believes. Go ahead, read the stories provided here and in the bonus material. I'm pretty confident the Holy Spirit can take it from there.

DISCOVERIES

If you want to nurture spiritual development in children, start here.

This core value will teach children to become aware of their own spirit and train them to hear God's voice. It will also help them understand the special connection between the Creator and His creation.

When children are in prayer training, the practice of listening is often overlooked. It is important for children to be trained to hear the Holy Spirit so that they may obey.

Listening for God's voice takes practice and discipline. However, in general, the younger the child, the more quickly he will sense (hear) things in his spirit.

A good biblical example is Samuel (1 Samuel 3). Samuel heard the voice of God, but it was Eli, his elder, who helped guide him to understand the experience.

IMPLEMENTATION: ADULTS

Adults need to be exposed to the fact that children can easily hear the voice of God once they are trained to listen for Him. And when children begin hearing His voice, adults should be prepared to act.

After the introduction of this concept, parents, teachers, and leaders need to begin asking children, "What has Jesus been saying to you lately?" Asking this simple question will build an expectation in them to hear from God.

Encourage families to schedule regular prayer times together. During these times, at the close of prayer, encourage them to "wait upon the Lord". Have them listen to: (1) know what He would have them do for that day or (2) understand the portion of Scripture that was shared.

If this material is new to your local church, consider hosting a voluntary training session for parents after receiving permission from appropriate leadership. Use this time to share your burden and give a brief overview of the plans you feel the Holy Spirit is guiding you to make.

Use corporate prayer times (prayer meetings, church services) to infuse children into the Body, giving them more practice time outside of a class or children's church environment.

IMPLEMENTATION: CHILDREN

Teach children (1) that they are spiritual beings living in earthly bodies, and (2) God—who is a spirit (John 4:24)—will most often communicate with them through their spirit, not through their natural senses such as hearing an audible voice.

Train children to listen with their spirit for the impressions, thoughts, pictures, words, and feelings, and little movies (visions) given to them by the Holy Spirit.

Make time for children to listen after a lesson to hear what the Holy Spirit is saying to them about how the lesson should be applied to their lives—individually and collectively. Too many times, teachers rush through the stories but do not have "impact time" for the children to really hear what the Spirit of God is saying to them. This is different from an altar call.

As children begin to practice the art of being still (quiet) in God's presence and learning to hear Him more clearly, some may find it difficult to "get anything," or "hear something." Reassure them that it's okay, and listen to the Holy Spirit for direction about how to proceed. Sometimes there is deep-seated doubt, or other distractions that can temporarily block the flow. Sometimes it is something as simple as the children needing background noise to help them focus. Quiet music can alleviate this problem.

Participate with children in sharing what you hear from the Holy Spirit during quiet times together. Sharing your personal, fresh encounters with Jesus will create a true bond with the children as you train them and build confidence.

When children "hear things in their spirit" that they do not understand, guide them to Scriptures or simply make note of their impressions and save them for a later time.

Sometimes children are like little "echoes." They repeat what they hear from someone else just so they can participate. This is good. Eventually, they will feel confident and comfortable to share their own personal experiences.

As a trainer, take on the challenge to encourage children and make them hungry for the supernatural working of the Holy Spirit.

It is important to build in listening times for impact and practice. These times don't just happen by themselves. Place a listening time strategically and allow enough time for your group to respond.

In most cases, children will enjoy the practice of listening and many will be excited about it, especially at first. Tap into their enjoyment to set a precedent for delight in prayer. When children realize God really does speak to them, listening can easily become one of their favorite times.

As you and your children become more comfortable sharing after listening times, you will discover that things come more quickly and clearly with practice.

CREATIVE IDEAS

1. Humans Are Spiritual Beings

A good way to teach this concept is to draw a comparison between an astronaut and a baby. In space, a person cannot survive without a special space suit. One can see the astronaut's suit but not the astronaut, the person inside.

Likewise, one can see a baby but not the spirit inside the baby. Our spirits make us who we are—our bodies are just outward "suits" needed to survive on this planet. Children are adept at living in the natural world, but they need to be taught about their spirit nature.

Understanding this powerful concept allows them to know that no matter what happens to the physical body through sickness, abuse, hunger, injuries or other events, the spirit is who they are on the inside and that is what Jesus is most interested in.

Parents and teachers train children in natural world tasks (i.e. tying shoes, helping with chores, feeding themselves), but seldom train children in the area of developing spiritual skills.

2. Other Spiritual Beings

All other spiritual beings are invisible unless they manifest themselves in some way on our planet. They would include God, angels, and demons/devils but do not include *ghosts* or animals. It is true, *we are not alone.*

3. Spiritual Ears

Draw a left and a right ear on heavy paper or cardboard; then cut them out. (You may prefer to purchase a pair of large, fake ears.).

Explain to children that their spiritual ears are in their midsection (stomach area). Hold the ears in your hands on either side of your stomach. This is the area where our feelings are felt most often. (If a child is afraid, where does he feel it? If he has done something good and is to be rewarded, where does he feel the excitement? If he is ever nervous, where are the *butterflies*?)

Feelings are an indication of where our spirit is (John 7:38). Therefore, we will often have a *feeling* about something we have learned from God's Word. It is one of the ways God communicates to us. You may find that younger children grasp this concept and begin hearing God speak to them through their spirits much easier than older children.

4. Can we listen for and hear God in our five senses?

Absolutely. Review the five senses (taste, touch, smell, hearing, sight) by doing things to engage each one. Ask children how these senses help them get around in the natural world. Then, ask them how these senses might help them in the spiritual world. Through this activity children will discover there are limited applications for using their natural senses in a spiritual world.

Many times, children expect God to speak to them through their natural senses. Though it is true God can use any of our senses to speak to us from time to time, let them know not to depend on them. These are senses we have learned to use in the natural world and work best in that environment.

5. Pictures, movies, and words in our mind

When God speaks to a person's spirit, the mind will often see little pictures or movies. At other times, a single word or sentence will be dropped into the spirit. These may have meaning for the moment, or for some future day. Children are very adept at using their "eyes of faith." Explain to them that this is another way they can recognize God speaking to them.

6. Journaling

Provide a notebook in which children can record their impressions and thoughts and other communications Jesus gives them. Some students may prefer to write and others will prefer to draw. The method thy use is an expression of their personality type and talents.

Explain to them that sometimes, what they hear may not make sense in the present, but to record it anyway because it may have meaning in the future. A journal is a great place to review what God has spoken to them, as well as an opportunity to record things when understanding comes. Reviewing these impressions over time is a great source of encouragement.

STORIES

Following are reports and excerpts of journals and drawings from activities in various churches around the world.

1. Listening Time United Message (New Zealand)

"He spoke to all of us that were in the room . . . the pictures and words that each of the children wrote and drew that day are amazing. The most incredible thing about them is that they are all very similar. They describe a portion of Scripture in Acts 2:17-21. The pictures are of the Church being rained down upon during the daytime while the sun is shining. Some of the church buildings are on grasslands, others are on the hills or on water."

2. Listening Time (Singapore)

In a training meeting, teachers at the Tabernacle of Joy had expressed their enthusiasm to learn more about how to lead a listening time. Several months prior to the training many of their children were exposed to a dynamic listening experience (told in the bonus material, page 154). These children literally begged their teachers to lead them in more listening times, but the teachers weren't sure what to do. So, they agreed that day to try it for themselves.

After a minute or so of waiting, they followed my simple instruction of "write or draw the first thing that comes to your mind when you close your eyes." Each person got one small thing, a piece to a larger message. As each teacher shared, piece by piece, the picture came together. The first teacher saw the number one in a circle. A few other teachers saw racecars or a car of some kind. Then, someone shared they saw a burst of light. Another saw a straight highway. Each piece emboldened the next person to contribute until the message was clear.

How they interpreted those pieces was: "Our kids are like a formula one racing car. They are ready to go forward and want to go forward speedily. We can't be afraid of the road ahead, but need to ride along with them.

What a confirmation!

3. Listening Time (Clearwater, Florida)

During their fist listening time, children drew many different pictures. As they shared them with the group, I noticed all of them included a tree, which was somewhat strange considering the varied content. One of the students noticed it too but none of us knew what the connection was.

In this case, we collected the pictures and showed them to their teachers during a subsequent training meeting. At first, no one seemed to get the connection. So, we waited, listening for a prompt from the Holy Spirit. Then, it was like a light bulb went off as one teacher understood the connection between all those trees and a sermon the pastor had preached the year before.

As she shared the connection, the entire group felt a confirmation as a wave of intercession for their children hit. The trees represented their children. With one exception, all the trees were bearing fruit in the pictures. It was a surprise to the teachers and they were both energized and humbled by the experience.

4. Journaling During Meetings (Bridgeton, Missouri)

Children were given permission to journal at any time during meetings, at a special location in the back of the room, known to them as a "Scribe's Desk". These are some of the things they wrote.

After singing a worship song: "A great pulse went through my body like I just exercised for ten hours. / The glory of God was just filling me up. It felt amazing. / I felt the presence of the Lord go through my body like cold water. / While we were doing the song "Holy, Holy," I felt God talking to me saying, "THANK YOU!" / When we were doing the song "Holy, Holy," I felt like God was talking to me and I felt really good. / When we prayed, I asked God where I should build my altar and God said, "I want you to build your altar at the end of your bed." Thank You, Jesus. / When we did the altars, I saw pictures of God and other angels."

During a prayer training session: "God told me, "I love you. I still care for you." I saw God on a cross with blood dripping down and God says, "I love you." / I felt something like going on a roller coaster for the first time. / I heard God say, "My servant." / God simply said, "I forgive you." / I saw a lighted circle in my eyes flickering and my stomach felt like I had butterflies in it."

5. Journaling After A Service (West Palm Beach, Florida)

"I felt a warm feeling in my heart. It was really hot. I think I felt Jesus inside of me. I felt like praying for people. Jesus was talking to me. It was great. / Jesus talked to me and said, "I love you." / I felt like the Lord came to me and said, "I love you, Karyna, come with Me to My kingdom. / I think God was telling me that if I get baptized I will be helped and that when someone is crying or something, I need to help them and pray for them and see their problem. That is what God said. / Today Jesus touched me and I felt something special. God has given me a lot of things, but I think I should give Him stuff back (spiritually)."

6. Journaling With Pictures

1. This picture represents the little babies that the devil is trying to kill through abortion in America. God said they're going to be okay. (Satan tried to rid the world of a deliverer when Moses was born and when Jesus was born too—his methods haven't changed.) The little girl said, "The crocodiles aren't going to win."

2. This picture shows how God kicked Satan out of heaven.

3. Sarah, a visitor to a kids' prayer camp, felt she was blooming with God after spending time learning about His love and power.

4. The following three pictures were drawn by children as a congregation prayed for their city. Pictures were then posted on a wall. After the prayer time, a gentleman came to the platform to share what he saw in his spirit; something like bombs exploding as they had prayed. At that point a parent noticed several children had drawn on paper what this man and others had seen as they prayed.

Pictures posted on the wall after a church prayed for their city.

Chapter 2: HOLY SPIRIT
Staying Full & Being Led

CORE VALUE – Mark 16:17-18; Acts 1:8

Mark: *These signs will accompany those who believe: They will cast out demons in my name, and they will speak new languages. They will be able to handle snakes with safety, and if they drink anything poisonous, it won't hurt them.*

Acts: *But when the Holy Spirit has come upon you, you will receive power and will tell people about me everywhere--in Jerusalem, throughout Judea, in Samaria, and to the ends of the earth.*

Several years ago, I asked myself, "What examples are there in Scripture of people who were full of the Holy Spirit?" This question sent me on a treasure hunt from Genesis to Revelation. I thought I knew the answers before I began, but much to my delight, I discovered some very interesting artifacts.

In short, what I discovered is that, people full of the Holy Spirit have a long and varied list of expressions of their fullness. In the past I have been guilty of fixating on one outcome or another, but the truth is, being full of the Holy Spirit produces a plethora of expressions. Prophesying, singing, dancing, edifying, worshipping, forgiving, speaking in tongues, blessing others, preaching, boldness, and even walking into a wilderness are expressions of fullness, and are recorded in Scripture. Incidentally, each expression is connected in some way to bringing glory to God.

So, when you are full of the Holy Spirit, what are you empowered to do? Sculpt, paint, administrate? Teach, witness, express love? Forgive, forget, remember? You fill in the blank.

It is interesting to note that not only are we empowered to *do* things, we are empowered to *be*. For me, someone who grew up with a desire to "work for the Lord," it was difficult to imagine that just *being* could be a product of the fullness of God's Spirit in me. Just *being*, without masks or excuses, is one of the most incredible proofs of how the Holy Spirit can fill all the gaps in a person's life. If you're looking for wholeness, you will find it in the Holy Spirit.

The Holy Spirit empowers us to be ourselves to the nth degree. That "you" you want to be is possible through the power of the Holy Spirit. Learning to stay full is your key to the life you've always wanted. From what I can tell, the Holy Spirit doesn't turn us into clones of Jesus, rather it helps us fulfill our destinies as Jesus fulfilled His. After all, Jesus was full of the Holy Spirit too (Luke 4:1).

The take-away for me has been the understanding that people will express their fullness in many different ways. Some of us will speak in tongues more than others. Some of us will prophesy. Others will sing, dance or express fullness through various forms of creativity. Some will be empowered to edify, preach, teach and all the other churchy things you can think of. And this is only the beginning of what a finite mind can fathom.

Unfortunately, being full doesn't always lead us in a rosy direction. Some of us will be led into a wilderness and into times of trying. Others will experience prison for His name's sake. Even others of us will give up our lives, careers, and reputations as we align ourselves with the work of the Holy Spirit in us. It's a good thing the power of the Holy Spirit is a comfort to us, especially when being full may mean walking a difficult path.

On the bright side, giving children a chance to understand these concepts and to express their true selves under the influence of the Holy Spirit is probably one of the greatest gifts we've been given as trainers. And, being able to lead them in the practice of staying full is perhaps one of life's biggest delights.

As you go through this essential, please bear in mind I'm not intending to give a full treatise on the work of the Holy Spirit, but rather, I am hoping to help you train children to understand the function of the Holy Spirit in their lives, through prayer. I am intentionally focusing on this one aspect of the Holy Spirit's influence in our daily lives.

Let's be full for Christ. All for One. One for all.

DISCOVERIES

Holy Ghost or Holy Spirit? You will notice that I refer to the Holy Ghost as the Holy Spirit in this handbook. To me, the terms are interchangeable and are simply a matter of preference. I began using the term Holy Spirit several years ago because I wanted to clearly tie the teaching about listening, to the work of the Holy Spirit. When I distilled my terminology, it seemed children were able to make a stronger, quicker connection to how a human spirit can communicate with God who is a spirit and vice-versa. For me, the transition from Ghost to Spirit was worth the effort.

A special gift? I've heard it said that not everyone is given the gift of tongues. And while I agree with this assertion whole-heartedly, I don't believe that the gift of tongues is the same as what happens when a yielded person speaks in tongues. Praying in the Spirit (with tongues) serves a purpose in our spiritual lives, five purposes, in fact. Without access to the power stream of praying in the spirit, it would be utterly impossible for these purposes to be met. Consider the five purposes below:

1. To provide a greater way of glorifying and worshipping Jesus
2. As a sign to unbelievers
3. As a "coded" prayer language
4. Building up my inner self
5. Impartation of power.

Contrary to what many people teach, the initial infilling of the Holy Spirit is an experience that is more than a "ticket to heaven." Comparatively speaking, perhaps a better word picture would be that of a passport. Jesus gives us a passport that opens up a whole new world, rather than simply handing us a ticket to a single destination that can only be used once in a lifetime.

Recorded examples in the New Testament of people filled with the Holy Spirit

1. John the Baptist—Luke 1:15
2. Elisabeth—Luke 1:41
3. Zacharias—Luke 1:67
4. Simeon—Luke 2:25
5. Jesus—Luke 4:1
6. First Church—Acts 2:2, 4; 4:8; 4:29-31
7. Stephen—Acts 6:3, 5, 8; 7:55
8. Paul—Acts 9:17; 13:9; 13:51-52; Romans 15:13-14; Ephesians 5:18-20
9. Barnabas—Acts 11:22-24

IMPLEMENTATION

Begin training in this area by providing time for intercession and praying in the Holy Spirit (tongues) for the needs of others. Time needs to be given for this in the home, as well as in the classroom or children's services.

Help children develop their sensitivity through "listening" for Jesus to give them a word, sentence, picture, movie, or feeling. Then release them to pray for the need, according to what has been revealed to them.

As a training method, encourage children to pray until they run out of words in their first language. When they don't know what to say next, they can then more easily allow the Holy Spirit to pray through them with words or sounds, even groans they don't understand. There is no need to worry about doing it wrong. No one around them will know the difference, because it is communication between them and God.

Help children understand that praying in tongues for a need is somewhat like praying in a secret code. Only God, or someone He has selected, can break the code. God's enemy, the Devil, doesn't have the cypher.

As an instructor/trainer, it will help considerably if you are comfortable switching to tongues as you nurture children to yield themselves to God. If you are uncomfortable doing this, consider practicing in a safe environment, and ask God to lead someone to you who can assist in this area.

Talk much and often to children about the Holy Spirit. Answer questions and follow the leading of the Holy Spirit in every matter concerning training. Children need to experience firsthand the power of the Holy Spirit, and they are able to enter in when someone is willing to guide them.

Tongues…Are You Kidding Me?

If you are unfamiliar or uncomfortable with the idea of people speaking in tongues, you're not alone, nor are you the first to question this supernatural phenomenon. I encourage you to take time to study people who were filled with the Holy Spirit at the birth of the New Testament church (Acts). Countless thousands living on the earth today have experienced it for themselves. It's not a fluke and it's not trickery. I can attest to the reality of it.

If you decide that tongues is not an experience for you, or you have reservations about training children to physically yield to the Holy Spirit, please consider putting this information out there for your children anyway. Lead them down this path to Jesus and let Him do the talking. It's not as spooky as you might think. And if you are of the persuasion tongues is a gift, please don't restrict it.

CREATIVE IDEAS

1. Who is in control?

In addition to the initial infilling of the Holy Spirit, children need to learn to live full of the Holy Spirit. Many times, when children are filled with the Holy Spirit, they speak in tongues in a highly emotional condition. This makes it difficult for them to grasp how the Holy Spirit can move on them or pray through them in a different environment, such as a quiet prayer time at home. Learning that they are in control, even when God's Spirit is moving on them, is empowering and demonstrates God's great love and respect for them.

How to jump the hurdle? The best way I've found is to do an exercise that encourages children to break through their self-consciousness. Children are often afraid that the way they pray is wrong, perhaps because it doesn't sound like the grown ups who pray around them. Stressing they can not mess up, because only God needs to understand their words and heart, can have a positive impact on their willingness to try.

Now for a few nuts and bolts. Make time for children to give praise to God in a limited amount of time, using words they know. When they run out of words, instruct them to keep their mouths open (don't close them). Perhaps even encourage them to make a small sound (so they won't close their mouth). Then, as the strange words begin to flow, melt into it.

If you interested in training children to yield to the Spirit at any given moment, do the above exercise, then stop them mid-prayer. Let them start back up again when you give a signal. Also, letting children use their inside or outside voice (on cue) will help them understand that they are yielded, but in control. This may seem a bit strange, but it is a practical way children can practice yielding to the Holy Spirit, without years and years of experience. No matter where children are or what conditions exist in their environment, they can pray in tongues in any situation.

The ability to slip between the natural order of this world, and the order of the world we cannot see, empowers us to obey when we hear something from God. Too many times, children who are Spirit-filled wait for the Spirit to move on them externally before they respond. Training children to yield, open their mouth, and get over their own self-consciousness, allows them to respond as the Holy Spirit moves in them.

It isn't good for any of us who are Spirit-filled to wait for extreme conditions or pressure to switch us over to a prayer language that is God-inspired. Being able to slip in and out of praying in the Spirit takes practice but is a key way we build up our inner man.

2. Hungry for the Supernatural

Kids who are hungry for the supernatural need to be made "hungry" for the Holy Spirit, so teach lessons and give testimonies of the power that comes from above, through this amazing gift from God.

A great object lesson is comparing a hand tool to a power tool. A hand tool, such as a screwdriver can accomplish much. It can help hang a picture or put a bookcase together. Likewise, praying with our own understanding for the world or someone in our life is a good thing, but may lack power. A power tool on the other hand, i.e. a power drill, can also help hang a picture or put a bookcase together, but in a fraction of the time. Additionally, it can do so much more. Yielding to God is a small price to pay to wield such power.

Children often struggle for recognition and respect because of their age and size. This is perhaps one reason why superheroes are so popular. In general, when exposed to these teachings about the Holy Spirit and when given a chance to practice, children love tapping into a source of power that respects their space, their ways, and their needs.

3. Praying in Code

Developing a prayer language, or praying in code, can greatly benefit any believer. Being able to pray in tongues is a great release of control to God's Spirit, especially in times of intense intercession and spiritual warfare. This is a different experience from the initial infilling of the Holy Spirit, at which time glorifying God is a key component, not necessarily doing battle.

The idea here is to convey information primarily about spiritual warfare. Yes, children are capable of spiritual warfare. The spiritual dynamic activated when they praise God is an indicator that they are capable and vital to God's strategies.

A great example to demonstrate how this works is via basic information about Code Talkers from World War II.

During WWII, Native Americans from the Navaho tribe were used in military service to send and receive coded messages in their native tongue. These men were great assets because no one else, anywhere in the world, understood their language. Locals from Hawaii were used in the Pacific arena for the same purpose—their Pidgin English couldn't be understood by the Japanese. This gave the United States an incredible advantage.

The Germans also used a secret code (enigma), but it was eventually broken because it was based on logic and a cypher that was eventually decrypted. This put them at a major disadvantage.

Applying this example to "praying in the Holy Spirit", or praying in tongues, is pretty obvious and most children will grasp it quickly.

When we pray in the Spirit, in tongues, we are praying in a kind of code that can be understood by God as we pray His will. This is important because of the nature of spiritual warfare and the reality of the dominion of darkness that shadows the lives of individuals, cities, states, and nations.

The more we practice, the easier it is to find this groove. The quicker we find the groove, the quicker we can be mobilized whenever and wherever there is a need. The ability for God's people, including children, to switch into this mode is crucial!

"For we are not fighting against people made of flesh and blood, but against the evil rulers and authorities of the unseen world, against those mighty powers of darkness who rule this world, and against wicked spirits in the heavenly realms" (Ephesians 6:12).

4. Variety, the Holy Spirit's Spice

Encourage children by recounting stories of how the Holy Spirit has led people that they may know personally. This involves "listening" and obeying as well as praying in tongues. It also involves forgiveness, worship, loving and so on. Refer to information on what is recorded in the New Testament about people who were full of the Holy Spirit.

5. Always Perfect

If a child has difficulty praying aloud, assure him that there is no wrong way to pray, especially in tongues, because nobody can understand him except God anyway. If all else fails, encourage him to try again when he gets home and is all alone.

6. Pressing In

When you've set aside time for a God Encounter or a Move of God (MOG) segment in your class, children's church, or home study, there will be times when people need to band together, as a group, to "press-in."

"Press-in" is simply a phrase that depicts the work it might take for the group to focus on God and get serious about what He wants for them. Pressing-in is a great word picture to help build momentum in a group as you lead them to Jesus, so He can speak with them directly.

Pressing in can take as little as a couple of seconds to as much as 10 minutes, but usually not much more; it depends on the need. Once there is a breakthrough, a release, it catches like wildfire. It can be short and intense, long and somewhat exhausting, or light and exhilarating. It all depends on where Jesus wants His children to go. Be prepared for anything.

STORIES

1. Uno, Dos, Tres

Little Lanae was so excited to tell her Sunday school teachers that she could pray in tongues any time she wanted to. She burst into the classroom one Sunday morning and said, "I can speak in tongues!" "Oh yeah?" her teachers replied. "Yup, watch".

"Uno, dos, tres." That was it. You can imagine the smiles on her teachers' faces. But at six years old, Lanae was beginning to make a connection. Today, she can switch into tongues without much effort when she prays, and I think it just might be because she has known it was possible for a very long time.

2. English Tongues in Africa

Vicki Simoneaux, a former missionary to Africa, has reported three occasions where people who have received the Holy Spirit in Africa, including children, spoke in English very clearly. In all cases, they were glorifying God and thanking Him for washing away their sin.

3. English Tongues in China

While visiting Central China, my dad was shocked to hear English spoken in a room full of Christians as the Holy Spirit fell during a prayer time in a secret meeting. It was his first personal encounter after hearing stories for years about this phenomenon. The man speaking in English was thanking God for washing him clean (like the African stories). My dad had been introduced to this man before service and had to communicate via interpreter, as he knew no English.

,. Spanish Tongues on Pacific Island

Former missionary to El Salvador, Bruce Howell, was preaching on an island in the Pacific when he heard someone speaking beautiful Spanish. He got near the woman who was speaking and discovered she was praising God. When she finished praying, he tried to converse in Spanish with her, but she looked at him like he was a bit crazy. As it turns out, she didn't speak or understand Spanish once she finished praying.

5. Tibetan Tongues in America

An elderly man in a prayer meeting in Michigan began praying softly, but fervently, in tongues for about ten minutes at the end of a prayer meeting. As the meeting closed, a woman at the back of the room stood and gave a testimony. She said, "I am a missionary and felt drawn to come into your church as I drove down your street tonight. This man was speaking in an obscure language I am familiar with from Tibet. He was praying for the release of a Chinese house pastor from prison, by name."

6. Easy Way or Hard Way?

During a Kids Camp altar call, children in large numbers were pressing in, focusing on Jesus. I noticed children at various stages of yieldedness to the Holy Spirit around me but one little girl caught my eye.

As she stood praying with hands raised, she was watching what appeared to be a very desperate boy nearby who was "seeking" for the Holy Spirit to fall on him. I could tell she was getting tired and she was nearly ready to quit "trying" for the evening.

I got her attention and asked her if she thought the boy would be filled before he went to bed. She just blinked, not knowing how to answer. "Do you want to be filled tonight before you leave here?" I asked. As she cast a quick glance toward the boy who was now pounding the floor with his fists, she sheepishly nodded yes.

Before I went further, I asked if she wanted to get filled with the Holy Spirit the easy way or the hard way. She chose the easy way, so I took a few minutes to explain she couldn't make a mistake or do it wrong. Then, I shared Cynthia's method of jumping off a cliff (explained in the bonus material, page 169) and off we went. After a few attempts at keeping her mouth open when she ran out of words to praise God with, she started rattling off praise in tongues. I could tell she was somewhat surprised at how easy it was as a smile spread across her face and she closed her eyes.

A while later, she was ready to go, satisfied and delighted with her experience. Why do something this wonderful the hard way? The easy way is a lot faster and leaves more time for other things, like fellowship with friends. As she walked away glowing, the poor guy nearby was still sweating it out the hard way. Sad thing is, I had tried to get his attention twice to help him, but someone had already convinced him it was supposed to be difficult.

7. The Clown's Method

Lloyd Squires, commonly referred to as The King's Clown by several generations, shared a similar style of helping children pass through the veil between the natural world and the spiritual one that was helpful to me.

He shared that, many times, when doing a group altar call or working one-on-one with a child, he would put a reasonable limit on their response time; telling children if they gave it all they had for the next five minutes, there would be extra time for playing afterwards. It may seem like a simple thing, but letting children know getting full of the Holy Spirit isn't a difficult affair built their ₓpectancy. Thousands have been filled as a result of his ministry. If the clown says it, it has to be true because the clown doesn't lie.

Chapter 3: WORSHIP
Silencing God's Enemies

CORE VALUE – Psalm 8:2
You have taught children and nursing infants to give you praise.
They silence your enemies who were seeking revenge.

If there is one essential capable of producing sheer delight for children (of all ages), I'm pretty sure this is it. The other essentials generate delight as well, but come with a small learning curve. With worship, it's plug n' play, baby. Plug n' play.

I'm inclined to share a story here that changed my life. It goes to demonstrate how you and I can directly influence children to be free or self-conscious in a corporate worship setting. It also gives you a peek at what a positive message reaping what you sow can be. I would contend that, if you are uncomfortable openly expressing your delight in God, whether with quietly falling tears or head-banging moves, this one's for you.

In 2006, at the East Coast Women's Conference, I was slated to present a session on kids prayer to over a thousand women. It was my first time to address such a large crowd, so I was extremely nervous. But there was one person who's behavior distracted me from my situation long enough to create intrigue, if not a little worship envy.

Barb Willoughby, the day speaker, was free styling on the platform. Then, due to lack of space, moved to the main floor during the worship service. We're talking, face up, arms akimbo, feet dancing, not just shuffling around. Barb and her husband

Steve, at that time missionaries in Singapore, had a reputation as worshippers and rightly so.

They had gone as far as to call the traditional "altar area" at the front of their church a "dance floor" during times of corporate worship. At the opening of services, they would announce, "The dance floor is open!" Reserved Chinese came forward and danced their way through a set of four or five songs before returning to their seats, streaked with sweat. I've been to Tabernacle of Joy and let me tell you, they really do live up to their name.

Back at the women's conference, Barb noticed her free stylin' way was attracting a lot of attention. As she spoke the first day, she addressed the gawkers and told us to, in her words, "Get your own dance." Notice how I used the word, "us?" I'll admit, she was talking to me.

As I got up to speak, things went well until, in the course of my remarks, I mentioned Barb's dance. Something in me tensed up and I blurted out my intention to "get my own dance." In front of that huge, intimidating crowd of women, I pledged to get my own groove. Afterwards, I remember thinking, one thing, "uh-oh."

As usual, when I returned home I shared what had happened with my kids prayer group. We were a bit stunted in the area of worship so it was time for me to step up. I issued a challenge. I dared my kids to worship in the open space in front of the platform of our local church. I promised if they went, I'd go too. This caused a ripple of laughter because they knew how klutzy I am.

What was I thinking? In the very next service, some of the kids who intended to take me up on my little dare sat in the same row with me. Their trash talk was working. They were saying, "Sister Angie, you're going down." I had butterflies the size of dinosaurs prancing around in my stomach. Thank you very much.

For all their bravado, when it came time to move out into the aisle they froze. Now what was I supposed to do? Lead them? That wasn't the deal.

So, I took a deep breath, motioned them to follow me out toward a wall. We ended up shuffling our feet to the rhythm of the music along a wall halfway toward the front. Not quite the goal, but on our way.

At our next meeting, we discussed how things went that night and came up with a plan to just meet in the front area at the beginning of service. I secured permission to try this experiment, made contact with parents about our change in plans and the rest is history.

Eventually this area became known as the "worship corner." Children would regularly meet there after pre-service prayer, to dance and truthfully, sometimes to play.

When I left my home church to live and work overseas, they were going strong. A while later, I returned and was invited to join them in the worship corner. As I danced around, face up, arms akimbo, feet dancing, it hit me how far I'd come from worship envy to freedom. That night, we had ourselves a ball.

I know expressive worship isn't all there is to this topic. But I wanted to let you know clearly that reaping what you sow can be a very delightful thing! And sometimes when sowing, it's not so much flinging seed as it is digging around in the ground, getting up close and personal with the truths you're trying to convey.

Best wishes planting seeds of worship. May your free styling days be full of delight!

DISCOVERIES

Worship is akin to complimenting. It is first noticing something good about God, and then expressing it in some way. God deserves this attention and we are blessed to give it to Him.

One of the most important things children can contribute to the Body of Christ is worship. Why? Because when they do, God's enemies are silenced.

Satan is known as the "accuser of the brethren," which means he is constantly trying to tattle on us, or make things up to get us in trouble with each other and ourselves. If he is silenced by the worship of children then his main weapon, his mouth, is useless.

There is no Scripture that promises results like Psalm 8:2 when an adult praises the living God. Therefore, training children to worship is a part of God's plan to deal with His enemies.

IMPLEMENTATION: ADULTS

Introduce adults to the core value via a Bible study or special meeting. Adults need to be informed if they are to change their thinking.

Sometimes cultural barriers need to be broken for the Bible culture to work.

Explain to teachers, parents, and church members that children need to be included in the body of Christ. In this way, children can use their energy and delight, even during play, to silence the voice of the enemy.

Incorporate ways for children to regularly worship corporately with the adults and youth, as it will help build respect between the generations.

IMPLEMENTATION: CHILDREN

You may want to do an introductory training session on the Body of Christ and what it means to be a part of it.

Teach Psalm 8:2 to children and allow them to put it into practice every time they meet for classes, prayer meetings, crusades, or other events. You want them to know the delight and sheer fun of worshipping God and that when they worship, something supernatural happens. Let them know that this is one way they can fulfill their role in the Body of Christ.

Introduce songs of worship that can be set to motion—let children worship with all their heart, mind, spirit, and body.

Let worship songs focus on "compliments" to Jesus for His great love, His sacrifice, and His wonders. Consider the current children's songs that are being sung; if they do not worship God, giving Him compliments, then do not spend as much time singing them. The power to silence God's enemies comes through true worship—not mere singing.

Teach children to understand that worship is not just singing at church. It is a way of making everything they do give glory to Jesus. Let children think about this and give answers as to what kinds of things they can do daily as worship. Make sure they understand the concept, "All of life is worship."

CREATIVE IDEAS

1. Visual Reminder

To reinforce the core value, occasionally allow children who are worshiping to place a piece of tape over the mouth of a stand-in for the Devil. Sometimes having a visual reminder brings the core value to their attention again. And, it's fun!

2. Using Music

Use worship songs, or at least one, before each class time begins to help children focus.

Allow children to help assign motions for some of the words or concepts of the songs.

Practice listening to lyrics and song speed. See if students can categorize songs according to whether or not they meet a "worship criteria" of giving God compliments.

Try worship without prerecorded music (rustic). Allow some of the children to form a percussion group. Make the worship time lively by marching or doing hand motions for songs.

Let children write praise and worship songs from Scripture, or share songs they hear in their spirit, that magnify Jesus. This is a very simple process and it is exciting to hear the beautiful thoughts and sounds they express. New songs are nothing new (Psalm 33:3, 40:3, 96:1, 98:1, 144:9, 149:1; Isaiah 42:10).

3. Training Worship Leaders

Nurture worship leaders so that you and other teachers don't have to do all the leading. Let children come to the front of the group to lead the worship time. Eventually, let children who show a propensity for worship plan the worship time. Make this fun and special by using real microphones and live music if possible. If that's not an option, prerecorded music, or favorite songs work great. No mics? Use sticks or even empty candy containers for microphones.

4. Developing a Worship Team

If interest is high and someone in your ministry group is gifted with creative expression, you may consider developing a worship team. This team would minister to children and adults through dramatic sign set to music, or some other form of specialized ministry.

Additionally, developing musicians and back-up singers may well be an outgrowth of an emphasis on complimenting God and ministering to others through music.

5. Making Space

Get permission to designate a worship area in the adult sanctuary where children can gather to sing and dance. Of course, this can include adults and youth also.

6. Worship Equipment

Waving banners during a worship service may not be common in your local church, but it is possible that children may be able to experience this Old Testament tradition in your class or children's church (Exodus 29:24).

Allow children to make small praise banners to use during worship time. These banners can be simple posters with praise words that they lift up to Jesus as they sing. Or they can be sticks with bits of string, ribbon, or fabric attached that children can wave before the

Lord. Paint sticks with crepe paper attached work great and are an inexpensive option to practice with.

Develop a number or alphabet system on small poster board to help kids change song motions for regular worship songs (fast usually). Assign each of four or five motions/moves to a number/letter. Let the kids pick and demonstrate each motion/move. Then, during worship, have a child hold up a poster when it is time for everyone to change from one motion or move to the next. This so much fun! Allow kids to assign new motions/moves to each number/letter weekly or as often as they would like.

7. Written Worship

Allow children to write worship prayers and read them aloud. Collect the prayers and use them from time to time to help give those who are shy a voice. Add to the written prayers until you have a worship collection. Then set the prayers to music—or let kids "rap" them.

8. Building an Adoration Alphabet

A fun way to get children to understand the idea of worship as complimenting God is to build an adoration alphabet. This is a simple activity that can be used occasionally through any stage of spiritual development.

Write one large letter of the alphabet on a piece of cardstock. Continue until there is one piece for each letter. Then, depending on your group size, come up with a plan for children to write or give input about complimentary words for each letter. A friend who tried this suggests laminating the cards for use with wipe-off markers for multiple use.

Don't try to do all the letters at once. Focus on a few at a time unless you have considerable time and personnel or are working with older children who could circulate through the 26 letters to add their choice.

Use certain letters or the set during group prayer times. Activities such as saying a prayer containing all the words on the card in one breath, or praying through the alphabet are great starter ideas. These are ultimately training exercises masked as fun activities.

All of these activities have been used in various settings in different countries around the world. I've tried them and others have tried them too. They are meant to be training activities that, in addition to generating worship, bring a group together and help children find their "voice."

STORIES

Clearly the most important aspect of this topic is doing it. Finding ways to get children to enter into authentic worship isn't as hard as one might think. See pictures on following pages.

GLOW, a kids worship team includes children as young as age 4 and up to age 12 or 13. GLOW stands for "God Loves Our Worship," and was thought up and adopted by children. GLOW ministers using dramatic sign enhanced by long sticks. They have ministered in their home church, conferences, and various other venues over time.

Inspired by the GLOW team, a group in Colorado begins to minister.

Worship equipment is such a beautiful sight.

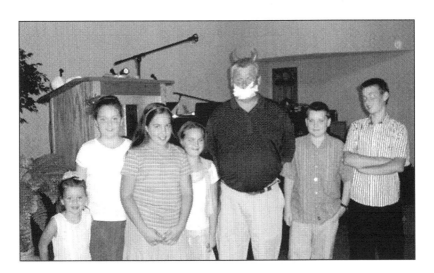

Silencing God's Enemies—a visual lesson.

Chapter 4: SCRIPTURE PRAYERS
Premeditated Prayer

CORE VALUE – Hebrews 4:12; Psalm 119:89

Hebrews: *For the word of God is full of living power. It is sharper than the sharpest knife, cutting deep into our innermost thoughts and desires. It exposes us for what we really are.*

Psalm: *Forever, O LORD, your word stands firm in heaven.*

Whether I am ministering in a small room, to a group of children in Bangladesh, or speaking at a kids prayer camp in Africa, I ask around to find out why children don't like to pray. Three answers pop up, across cultural lines. They aren't original. In fact, you've probably heard them before.

First, children don't like to pray because they don't know what to say or pray about. (This was addressed extensively in chapter two.) When we don't know what to pray, the Holy Spirit can pray through us. Another part, kingdom praying, will be touched on in the next chapter.

Second, children have told that me they don't like to pray because they don't really want to sound like the grown-ups around them. (This issue is addressed in chapter seven, page 99.) We each have giftings, personalities and talents that affect who we are and how we pray. Respecting these giftings releases us to communicate with God in a manner that is a good fit for us.

Third, children don't like to pray because they don't feel they will ever be good at it. They don't pray well, and few teachers can really nurture them to success.

Some teachers quote the Lord's Prayer as a model; others refer to a prayer sandwich, giving children a formula to follow. Though I'm not much for formulas, I've used them and taught them as a type of prayer training-wheels in the early days. I concede that they work, to an extent. However, they aren't dynamic enough to handle a God who is interested in a close daily relationship.

So, how do we nurture children to "pray good?" One way is to train them to pray in the language of the Bible. There are many prayers recorded for us as examples, we just have to research them, and perhaps present them in a translation that would be easy for children to understand. Unpacking prayers of the Bible can be an interesting on-going project.

We also nurture children by providing opportunities to use what they have been trained to do. For some, writing out their prayers in a premeditated way helps them dig down deep to get a handle on using this powerful spiritual weapon. Children can wield this weapon against any spiritual foe, from sickness to darkness and everything in-between. This tends to work extremely well for those who are a bit shy.

We can nurture them by encouraging them to practice actually praying the Word aloud. If you can't imagine what this sounds like, you may have to take my word for it up front; it is glorious!

The first time I heard someone pray Scripture over a congregation my eyes popped open and I soaked it all in, writing the prayer down as quickly as I could. It was the most beautiful thing I'd ever heard. Four Scriptures were woven together and spoken over us in such a way that my heart both melted and burned within me.

In my desire to replicate this quality in my own life, I stumbled across an excellent curriculum, Shekinah Kids, to help children do just this.

As you might imagine, having a curriculum wasn't enough. I had to solicit children who were interested. Then, once I had a group together, they had to be released to use what they had learned. Slowly, testimony by testimony, children gained courage to use what they had been trained to do. As a result, lives were changed, including mine.

As a facilitator, I was constantly on the lookout for safe and challenging growth opportunities for my group. If you're looking to nurture this essential in your children, you can most likely expect to do some advocating and making space for your children to minister.

A word about implementing this essential. It may be better to start by making it a voluntary endeavor. Save yourself the headache of age and behavior issues by training only those old enough and interested, even if it is a small number. Over time and exposure, others will get their curiosity piqued and willingly join.

Whether praying the Word off the top of their heads, or reading from a premeditated prayer written out beforehand, children can benefit greatly from learning the language of the Bible as they wield this great offensive weapon. The end result is something of great beauty, a delight to see.

To Mentor Or Nurture?

On a side note, you may have noticed I've used the word "nurture," quite a bit as opposed to "mentor." I make this distinction because after reading Lisa Bevere's book, "Nurture," I can appreciate the difference.

To boil it down, mentoring my children means duplicating in them something that is in me. Nurturing them, on the other hand, means finding ways to bring out what is in them.

Nurturing, rather than mentoring, is an active way I remind myself that it's not about me. I want my children to go farther than I've been and they can't do that if they are following me, walking in my footsteps. I prefer to help them follow Jesus; the fact that I get to travel with them is awesome.

I'm not sure if I have a favorite essential, but I really do like this one. I hope you do, too. I trust as you nurture children to speak the language of the Bible and pray prayers inspired by God's Word, you'll see more of Him reflected in them than ever before.

So, here's to miracles of healing and salvation; to blessed finances and expressions of delight in Jesus.

DISCOVERIES

Praying Scripture is a powerful way to apply God's written Word to our lives.

Scripture praying is speaking out the will of God. His Word is as right as it is eternal. Those who struggle with understanding the will of God for their lives can greatly benefit from praying Scripture which is His will in written form.

Reading and meditating on Scripture is a good practice, but speaking the eternal Word of God aloud causes things to happen in the spirit realm. The spoken Word of God is powerful when mixed with faith.

The Word of God is the Sword of the Spirit (Ephesians 6). It's an offensive weapon. Jesus used it effectively in the wilderness to parry blows from Satan who came to tempt Him.

When children begin to pray Scripture, they are taking part in the prophetic element of the Body of Christ, which in itself, is fulfillment of Joel 2:28, *"your sons and daughters will prophesy."*

IMPLEMENTATION

Choose passages of Scripture that deal with topics such as offerings, healing, salvation, forgiveness, power, blessing, and adoration. Train children to pray the content of the passages as short one-or two-sentence prayers. Here are a few ideas to help you get started. Look up the verses, and then compare them to the following one or two sentence prayers.

1. **Blessing/Adoration: Nehemiah 9:5**—Lord you give life to everything and the multitudes of heaven worship You!
2. **Protection: Isaiah 54:17**—God, your Word says that no weapon formed against [name] will prosper. Please keep him/her safe from the plans of your enemy. In Jesus' powerful name, amen.
3. **Offering: Mathew 11:28-30**—Jesus, you said anyone who is weary should come to you and you would give them rest. Use this offering to help many find your rest.
4. **Faith/Power: Hebrews 4:12**—Father, I thank you that your Word is living and powerful! I trust in your Word!

Train children to find their own topics by using a concordance like the one found in the back of most Bibles. After choosing a topic, have children practice writing their own prayers based on Scripture.

Give children opportunity to pray these Scripture prayers in corporate prayer settings (with other children or adults). Feature children who pray Scripture as often as possible so they can use what they are learning immediately.

Memorizing is good, but understanding content is most important. Being able to pray the content of Scripture back to God is just as powerful as quoting Scripture because in learning to pray content, children learn to apply the Scriptures to their personal lives.

Each child needs his own Bible to begin personally applying the principles of praying Scripture. Until he has his Bible or has access to one in his home, he will need to rely on materials provided by the church/class/teacher.

CREATIVE IDEAS

1. Using a Concordance

Show children how to look up verses by topic or key word by using a concordance. Then have children write out a simple one or two sentence prayer that prays that topic back to God.

For students who enjoy this type of work, allow them to find two or three verses on the same topic, then write a full prayer that incorporates the various aspects of each verse into one thought.

2. Shekinah Kids Curriculum

On heavy paper, create Scripture cards of sample one-sentence prayers prayed from Scripture. Include on each card the reference and a key word that will help identify it in the future. Allow students to make their own sets or make enough Scripture cards for your group to have a variety to choose from.

Develop a tracking system for keywords, assigning point values for cards completed and cards prayed during training time or external activities. Prepare small, medium and larger prizes (such as a nice Bible with concordance) so children will stay self-motivated for short, mid and long-term goals. Eventually the points don't matter as much as the opportunity to use what they have learned.

To assist with this idea, a curriculum complete with laminated cards, a tracking system, and detailed instructions is available from M'Linda Barnes via her website, www.shekinahkids.com. There are various pricing and material options to choose from, so you can tailor the program to your needs. After extended weekly use during a voluntary kids prayer training class, I can vouch for the effectiveness and value of these resources.

3. Extra Curricular Activities

Allow children to pray over the offering in a class, children's church or adult service. Encourage them to use Scripture prayers as well as prayers they have premeditated (written out).

Provide opportunities for children to lead in worship by opening a class, meeting, or service with adoration and blessing prayers.

4. Train As You Go

If this area of your life isn't as developed as you'd like, don't be afraid to train as you go, sharing what you learn with the children you lead. In the bonus material, you will find resources to help you in your personal journey of praying the Word.

STORIES

1. Prayer Training Class

During a regular kids prayer class, a visiting minister stopped in as an observer. He had heard about the class and wanted to see for himself how kids were learning to pray Scripture.

It was a busy and somewhat noisy night. Kids were working in pairs, racing against the clock to earn thousands upon thousands of points. He noticed the boys were working as hard as the girls, which rather surprised him.

In the final minutes of the class, he heard something that influenced his opinion of this concept beyond any testimonial I could give.

As I gave the thirty second warning before everyone had to stop for the evening, the minister noticed two boys who were feverishly finishing up their Scripture cards. One of the boys said, "Ooh, I have just enough time to finish this one." And he did just that. That statement, combined with the excitement and buzz of the class, sold him that night on the concept of kids prayer training.

It wasn't long until he invited the Shekinah Kids group to his office to pray for everything that went on there. His one night at kids prayer training led directly to two prayerwalks at his work place, an invitation for one of the kids to pray at a national function, an overseas trip and the spreading of the kids prayer message to another region of the world.

2. A Legacy of Premeditated Prayer

Larissa really got hooked on prayer when she was just nine years old. By age ten, after a teacher showed her how to look up verses and write her own prayers, she had prayed a prayer that led her mother to heath and her father into a job.

At age eleven, Larissa prayed a prayer of salvation for her grandpa, who returned to Jesus on his deathbed. At age twelve, though shy and shaking in her boots, she stood before 18,000 young people gathered at the 2005 National Youth Congress and prayed a simple, premeditated prayer of blessing over them.

Larissa didn't stop there. Well into her teens she taught sessions on Scripture praying at various kids prayer events, and energized a younger generation to do something new with God.

When Eunice, a 12-year-old girl in Guatemala heard of Larissa's premeditated prayers, she began to use Scripture to write out premeditated prayers of her own. Shortly thereafter she was asked to open the annual Guatemalan General Conference with a simple premeditated prayer of blessing; something that had never happened before.

Though seemingly unrelated, this connection served to spur Larissa on. As she entered high school, her burden for orphans, and willingness to use what she knew, led to an invitation to visit a newly opened orphanage in Guatemala. That trip sealed the deal for her. The compassion she felt toward orphans was something to pay attention to and not just some crazy dream.

There isn't an end to her story in sight. At the time of this writing she is in college, earning a medical degree to enable her future ministry to orphans. Pretty cool what God can do with someone who finds a way to connect with Him personally at a young age.

Chapter 5: KINGDOM PRAYING
It's All About Him

CORE VALUE – Matthew 6:33
And he will give you all you need from day to day if you live for him and make the Kingdom of God your primary concern.

I just didn't get it.

Growing up, my mental prayer list focused on family members, tests, and an occasional concern outside of myself. Though I'd been baptized at age four, and had spoken in tongues three years later, nothing much changed in me. I knew facts, Bible stories, and life applications for even the obscure Bible stories. But I was still a bit hard in my spirit. I was dedicated, but not very open.

Missions stories are what melted my heart. Some of my favorites were, and still are about Corrie Ten Boom, Nicky Cruz, and God's Smuggler (Brother Andrew); the trifecta of 70's gospel lore. My mother nurtured this interest by feeding me every scrap she could find and it made me even hungrier. I wanted what these people exhibited. In today's language, we would call what they had an "authentic relationship" with God.

I wanted it, but I still didn't get it. I was stuck until I realized my problem was that I wanted *what* they had, not *who* they had.

For nine years I worked and rubbed shoulders with some of the most incredible missionaries on the planet, including my parents. It seems that God inserted me into a living narrative to cause me to understand that I needed to go from a *what* to a *who* focus in my relationship with Him. I had stumbled through most of my life making things about what I wanted or needed, not about who He is or what He wants. I was intently studying the small picture, when He wanted me to get a glimpse of the big one. I was well over due for the great migration from "Me-ology" to "Thee-ology."

Ooooh! Now I got it.

That migration is the gist of Kingdom Praying, in a nutshell. It's going from what matters to me in this moment, to what matters to an eternal God who delights Himself in me. It is a way of living that puts God first, even in our prayers. This isn't to say we can't pray or shouldn't pray for our needs; it's just that we can trust God enough to put those things in the caboose of our prayer train.

It was shortly after my friend, Lisa Marshall, shared the idea of Kingdom Praying with me, that I found myself suffering from a reoccurring stomach problem. In an effort to apply this new understanding of putting my needs at the back of the line, I gave Lisa a call and told her my situation. She offered to pray for me right there on the phone, but asked which two countries I would like her to pray for first. I chose Chile and Turkey, as they are loosely linked gastronomically to my trouble spot. She prayed for them, then for my healing. Within minutes I was fine.

I realize that it's an anecdotal story at best, but it shows how simple faith in a Biblical truth just...works. I've tried just about every kind of Kingdom Praying strategy, even intentionally not praying for something I really want just to see if God takes care of my stuff when I put His stuff first. It must make Him crazy happy because He does.

Not long after I started teaching English in China I realized that my particular kindergarten was responding faster than normal to English education. I chose this as my test-imony. I believed my school could reach the number-one spot within five years, but I decided not to ever ask for it in prayer. Crazy? Maybe. But, it was my conscious decision to put God's things first, and in this case, to never ask Him for this dream.

He knew I wanted it. He heard me talk, plan, teach, study and network. And for whatever reason, perhaps for this paragraph, He caused it to happen. Upon finishing year five, my school snagged first place. And as if that wasn't enough, we snagged it by a wide margin. He did that for me. A small thing. And I never had to ask.

From this and so many other more mundane examples in my life, I can tell you with assurance that we can fling ourselves into full-throttled prayer on behalf of what He wants, knowing that He will come through on His promise. Doesn't He always? We can put Him first in our decisions about time, money, talent, even prayer. And when we do; His delight in us sees to the little things that make us delight in Him.

It's pretty safe to say that God is not trying to blow us away with His mighty acts, or bore us with His never-changing ways. However, He is interested in finding people in whom He can delight, so they can reflect His delight back toward Him. So, go ahead, put Him first in everything.

Try it. You'll like it. And so will He.

DISCOVERIES

When children pray for others, they are answering the only prayer request of Jesus, found in Matthew 9:37-38: *"He said to his disciples, 'The harvest is so great, but the workers are so few.'" So pray to the Lord who is in charge of the harvest; ask him to send out more workers for his fields.'"*

Training children to pray for what matters to God first helps them stop thinking only of themselves. It helps weed out selfishness and encourages them to prefer others ahead of themselves.

When children begin to put the Kingdom of God first in their prayers, they will begin to put the Kingdom of God first in other areas of their lives as well. Other areas may include finances, time, service, and social awareness.

Training children in this area produces people who see the sick and care for them, people who feed the hungry, and people who care for orphans and widows. Do not be surprised if, when children begin praying for the kingdom, they become interested in doing something to help others in need.

IMPLEMENTATION

Children need to understand that praying for others who have yet to hear the gospel message is part of what Jesus asked His followers to do.

Make sure children know that when they put God's things first, like praying for lost people groups or individuals, He will look out for them.

Be aware that children cannot pray for things they do not know about. You need to become informed, so the children you are training can become "informed intercessors."

Informed intercession leads to the fulfillment of Revelation 7:9. *"After this I saw a vast crowd, too great to count, from every nation and tribe and people and language, standing in front of the throne and before the Lamb. They were clothed in white and held palm branches in their hands".*

Children like to hear about the condition of children from other countries, even villages, that are different from their own.

This is a kind of praying that "shapes the world" because it is bigger than one's personal, church, village, or country's needs. It is praying for others first.

There are several areas of focus:

1. The 10/40 Window

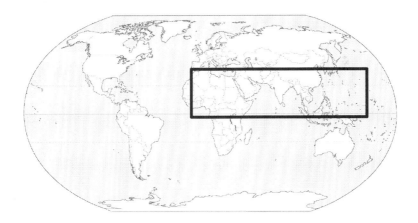

The "10/40 Window" is an area of the world that has the most people living in it, but the fewest Christians and/or missionaries. It is located 10 degrees north of the equator, and runs up to 40 degrees north of the equator. It spans an area from Korea through northern Africa and includes Indonesia.

This area was mapped out for Christian prayer groups in the early 1990's. As the A.D. 2000 movement gained steam for worldwide revival at the close of the 20th century, they used this simple idea to help rally the troops for a truly global initiative. Though the A.D. 2000 movement has come and gone, there is still much to be done in the "Window Nations."

In addition to housing the largest population geographically, the 10/40 Window is also a religious stronghold, resistant to the gospel message. Five of the world's largest religions and non-religions are located there. These people groups are: Tribal, Hindu, Unreligious, Muslim, and Buddhist.

2. THUMB-O

Initially, this idea was adapted from material put out by the Caleb Project in the early 2000's. THUMB-O prayers help children pray for particular people groups by religion; breaking down religious strongholds mostly found in the 10/40 Window. Even after nearly two decades of focused prayer, and after much progress, strongholds still exist.

THUMB-O prayers cover the major religions found in the 10/40 Window, with the addition of "O" for orphans. I have found the plight of orphans to be a very tender spot for children in any country.

3. Children At Risk

This segment of society covers a larger percentage of the world's population that one might imagine. Following are four areas of concern to get you started. Others can be found by doing a web search for topics listed on the UNICEF website.

Child labor is a major problem in developing nations. It keeps children from getting an education and continues a cycle of poverty and crime. Approximately 16%, or 150 million children, in developing nations are involved in harmful or exploitive labor. For more info, visit www.unicef.org.

Child soldiers are being forced into military roles at increasingly younger ages. "Today, as many as 300,000 children under the age of 18 serve in government forces or armed rebel groups.

Some are as young as eight years old . . . orphans and refugees are particularly vulnerable" (www.hrw.org—human rights watch organization). As of 2012, child soldiers are actively fighting in at least 14 countries.

Orphans, street children, and child refugees all need prayer for protection, provision, and the love of Jesus. (For example, in sub-Saharan Africa some 500,000 children under the age of fifteen died of AIDS in 2004, according to the United Nations. This is in addition to the large number of children orphaned due to the AIDS virus around the world.)

Unborn children, who are not wanted by their mothers, are at a high risk of being aborted. The numbers stretch well into the millions.

CREATIVE IDEAS

Following are tried and true favorites to get you started. Volumes of other ideas, newer ones perhaps, may be found easily by visiting www.kidsprayer.com. This website, run by the World Network of Prayer, is the most robust, information-packed and resource-filled kids prayer website available. Another great thing about this site is that the person posting the material actually leads a kids prayer initiative.

1. Get Global!

(This idea was one of the first missions prayer ideas I saw demonstrated by kids prayer advocate, Esther Ilinsky.)

Allow children to toss a globe from person to person in a circle. Wherever their index finger lands, is the country/place that they pray for. If a lightweight globe is not available, make one from materials at hand. (Draw continents on a ball, or balloon.) Children say, "Get global!" as they toss the ball/balloon to one another.

Ideas for prayer include children at risk and "children like me"—those who wear glasses, those with red hair, and so on.

2. 50/50 Prayers

Children with prayer requests get a partner. The partner prays for them; then the child with the request prays for others in the world with the same need. This can be done simultaneously, in a group, or pair by pair in front of the group. Doing this pair by pair is a good way for other children to learn how to apply ideas for their own prayers.

3. Prayer Spinner

Sometimes, a group children tend to pray for the same things over and over again, perhaps because their minds go blank. Maybe some day there will be an app for this, but for the time being, using a prayer spinner keeps things interesting. (Any programmers out there want to take the bait?)

I highly recommend purchasing a set of durable spinners like the ones offered by kidsprayer.com. However, if you need something in a hurry and don't have time to wait for your new spinners to arrive, consider trying this.

Write ten kingdom needs on a flat surface in the shape of a circle (pie). Here are some examples: (1) unity, (2) a country, (3) catch the vision, (4) others like you, (5) Holy Spirit, (6) 10/40 Window, (7) praise and thank God, (8) others, (9) unreached children, and (10) families. Grab a marker, empty soda bottle or something similar to serve as the spinner. Place the spinner in the middle of the circle, then, give it a spin. Wherever it lands is what children (or a child) pray for.

One boy used a paper plate, divided it into segments, and then wrote prayer ideas he liked. He would close his eyes, spin the plate, and wherever his finger pointed would be his prayer focus.

4. Praying While Playing

These ideas are from local kids prayer groups. What is the most popular toy your children play with? Can it be used to help them pray in some way? Let children be a part of the creative process as they pray while playing.

A. Ball

Write kingdom requests around the ball and instruct children to roll it to one another. Whatever request is facing up is a child's prayer focus.

B. Rope

Children pray while they jump rope individually or as a group.

C. Tops/Spinners

Designate at least four kingdom needs for each direction—north, south, east, and west. Spin a top and whichever way it is pointing when it stops spinning, that is the prayer focus. Letting two tops go at the same time can also be fun—the child whose top stops first, prays first.

5. Maps

Use maps of all sizes for children to pray over. Let children use their hands to touch different countries, perhaps even laying on them to "cover" them in prayer.

6. Candy

10/40 Window: Use M&Ms to help train kids to pray for others. Link a people group to each color. Let kids come up with various ways to pray for each people group using the M&M colors. Suggested colors/groups: Brown/Tribal, Red/Hindu, Yellow/Unreligious, Green/Muslim, Orange/Buddhist, and Blue/Orphans.

> **Types and Colors:** Use various kinds of colored candies for similar activities, posting a color guide if necessary. Also, use different kinds of candy. For example Skittles, red licorice, gummy bears, etc. to promote various creative prayer focuses.

7. Light

To change things up, try using an inverted light activity. Children love being in a semi-dark environment on occasion (not too dark, especially for younger children). Use this technique to focus children's attention on how God's Word is a light in the world. Lead children to pray against spiritual darkness and for there to be light in the lives of people in their town, village, city and country. Key verses to consider are:

Psalm 18:28, 27:1, 36:9, 43:3, 56:13, 84:11, 89:15, 104:2, 112:4,119:105, 119:130 / Matthew 4:16, 5:14-15 / Mark 4:21 / Luke 1:78-79, 2:32, 11:36 / John 3:21, 8:12, 12:36a, 12:46

8. Newspaper

Praying for the homeless can help turn children's prayer focus away from distant countries and to someone they may have passed on their way to your class. Many times, it's easier to pray for a problem somewhere else than it is to pray about something under our own noses. To prepare students, do a little homework.

Find out about homelessness in your town or city, and share the information with the children so they can understand the need.

If you don't have homeless people wandering the streets of your small town, talk about how the economy has affected families recently and the struggles some are having. This may be an opportunity to give thanks, as much as to pray for those who need help.

Break children up into pairs or groups of three or four. Have one person lay on the floor, and the other person or group members cover him/her with newspaper. Take turns praying for the homeless, then switch places and repeat. (If the weather permits and temperatures are reasonably chilly, but not dangerously cold, you may consider doing this outside in winter, leaving coats inside.)

9. Online Resources

There are many ways to get information about praying for the harvest, as Jesus asked. There are vast online resources. However, I will point out just a few that I have found extremely helpful and cite my reasons for including them.

A. kidsprayer.com

This is my number one choice for articles and information as it is devoted specifically to helping kids prayer leaders. It has been in operation since the spring of 2004, and is chock full of new ideas, new materials, and articles with feedback. An experienced ministry leader keeps the content and design fresh and relevant. Plus, their store has a growing number of goodies to choose from.

As a bonus, they promote an annual kids prayer conference as well as a bi-ennial national prayer conference that includes a kids prayer track. Check the website for more.

B. kidsinministry.org

This is like the Swiss-knife of dynamic kids ministry websites. It is loaded with curriculum for purchase designed to lead children into a deeper walk with Christ. Many of the concepts I gleaned while using several of the curricula peep through in the 7 Essentials. The ministry also hosts annual training events.

C. joshuaproject.net

This site is great for getting information on people groups, especially unreached groups. Loaded with information and resources, they even have apps for iPhone and Android devices.

D. samaritanspurse.com

This is the home site for "Operation Christmas Child". Shoeboxes, filled with gifts for children, are sent around the world at Christmas. There are many ways children can get involved with helping other children through their kid-friendly sponsorship programs.

It is also a good place to check for news regarding national and international disasters, and their humanitarian responses to them.

E. worldvision.org

This website is run by a trustworthy organization that has been helping children and communities in underdeveloped nations for over half a century. If your children are touched by the plight of others, you may consider sponsoring a child as a group. There are other groups out there that do something similar, but World Vision goes a step beyond them. Not only do they physically help people and communities, but they also help emotionally and spiritually and are dedicated to spreading the gospel.

F. invisiblechildren.com

A great resource for trendy, catchy, and content-rich material. This site has a young-vibe! Videos, stories, and accessories are available for free and purchase at this site. Also, annual activities connect people from all over the world. There are even opportunities for group and individual involvement.

G. traveltheroad.com

These guys are hard-core, modern day missions-story makers. They travel the world on a shoestring budget, preaching anywhere they feel led to go. Their videos and photography are amazing. However, not all content is suitable for young children.

STORIES

Here are some stories about how kingdom praying has impacted kids in various settings in the church and family.

1. Lanae: From Prayer to Service

In a first grade Sunday school class: After four Sundays of focusing on praying for the world and simple one-sentence prayers in a repeat-after-me style, Lanae volunteered to do her own prayer (finally!). It changed the dynamic of the group and kids began saying their own prayers.

Eight years later, Lanae began teaching kids prayer in the three and four-year-old class of her local church and began attending seminars to be more fully equipped to train younger children. As of this writing, Lanae has earned a Bachelor's degree and is working on her Master's in a field she can use to help others. I have no doubt she will be the answer to some of her own tear-filled prayers from so many years ago.

2. Tyler: From Prayer to Action

Tyler, who was raised with a kingdom-praying emphasis at church and at home, raised his own budget and went on his first mission trip to Bangladesh at the age of twelve (with his dad). He continued to grow and train in areas of leadership and at the age of fourteen took his third mission trip to Bangladesh—this time with his entire family. As of this writing, Tyler is still going strong, gaining real life experience as he ministers through music.

3. Zack: Inspired

Zack, inspired by the praying-while-playing training, went home and designed his own prayer tool. He wrote the needs that most touched his heart on the sections of a volleyball. Then he got his mom and little sister to pray with him by rolling the ball to each other, praying for whatever need was facing up at the time. He was six years old. Since then, Zack has grown up helping whenever possible with kids prayer related activities and events.

4. Intercession Break Out

During a regular kids prayer training class, intercession broke out after the crisis of African AIDS orphans was explained. Parents had to wait for their kids to stop praying before going home. For

several months afterward, there were planned "inte
nights twice a month at the request of the kids.

5. A Pastor's Wife

Carla, a pastor's wife who began encouraging her Sunday school teachers to focus on prayer, was excited to report: "Even our teachers are excited about teaching, now that they train kids to pray for the world. There is so much they can do and the kids are really responding to it."

6. Boys Who Pray

Jen and her husband worked with fourth and fifth-grade boys during Wednesday nights at church. For years it seemed they were losing the boys; they did not like the Bible study part of the program at all. Even though their behavior told Jen they did not know the points from the Bible study, the boys often said, "We already know all that stuff!"

Jen wrote, "So when I came across your Web site, I decided to take a break from the curriculum we had and try something new that would stress something we did see a twinkle of hope in— prayer. Those boys can pray! We have been going through the M&Ms for Missions and THUMB prayers. It is Bible study and action all wrapped up in one!

"It is wonderful! The Lord is good! These boys know they can have an important role in the kingdom. Thanks!"

7. Soldiers Stopped

During an intense intercession time for the protection of children in Uganda, something really special happened. In an intense three minutes of prayer, children saw in their mind's eye the feet of soldiers in the light under a door. They saw the feet move away from the door and "heard" their guns jam and feet run away.

The night they prayed was the morning in Uganda when rebel soldiers and government forces made a tentative cease fire agreement. It hit the news in America the following day. Children came to the next kids prayer time delighted to tell how they could see what God was doing and were ready to do more.

Chapter 6: HEALING

In His Steps

CORE VALUE –John 14:12; James 5:15

John: *The truth is, anyone who believes in me will do the same works*
I have done, and even greater works, because
I am going to be with the Father.

James: *And their prayer offered in faith will heal the sick, and the Lord*
will make them well. And anyone who has committed sins
will be forgiven.

I don't know why God chooses to heal some people instantly or through their doctors and why sometimes He chooses not to. I don't think I'd ever be able to figure it out, if I tried and tried. There. I'm glad I got that off my chest. I just wanted you to know that up front, before you read any further. I would hazard a guess that we're in the same boat.

It was me he came to that first night during ministry time, asking for help. He asked me to find a couple of kids to pray for him. His name was Stan. He had a brain tumor and wasn't doing well. As I stepped away to rustle up a few kids, you can believe I was inwardly crying out for guidance from the Holy Spirit every step.

I was led to two girls, two powerhouses in prayer. They were young and untested, and I was unsure. But they weren't afraid to pray for Stan. In fact, they were eager when they discovered that someone had invited them to pray. So, we went to Stan together, they put their hands on him, worked through the L.A.B.B. Method questions and responses (covered later in this chapter, page 91) then set to prayer. It was an intense few minutes; and I was holding my breath the whole time. "Now what," I thought. Nothing appeared to have happened. The girls smiled and wandered off, seeking their next target to bless.

The next weekend, Stan caught the eye of those same two girls during ministry time and they made a beeline toward him, prayed intensely for him and hugged him goodbye. Within a few weeks, a pattern emerged. The girls would go to Stan first, pray for him, and then make their way to others.

They never shied away from him, even when things got bad. They prayed for him first, smiled at him, and pretty much poured out love on him. And on nights when he was too sick to attend, they would ask prayer for him, on their own, from the other kids. After a year of this, Stan was declared cancer free. Stan credited his recovery to those two little girls.

Right about the time Stan was declared cancer free, the grandpa of one of the girls, Cynthia, passed away. She had been praying for him for a long time as well. It didn't make sense to any of us why her prayers for Stan brought healing and her prayers for her grandpa didn't.

At this point, if you're expecting a sermonette on the sovereignty of God, hang on there's more.

To make things worse, Cynthia told me she knew her grandpa was going to be made whole. She said God promised her. At first I didn't really know what to tell her. So, I chimed in saying I didn't understand either. As you can imagine, over the next several days, I spent some quality time asking God what was going on. "If I am going to lead children to pray for others in this way, I need answers," I prayed.

And then I heard Him. He did speak to Cynthia and He didn't lie. Here are a few things He wanted me to know.

When we get a Word from God that someone is going to be whole or well, we need to proceed with an understanding that He isn't bound by time. Perhaps what God is intimating is that the person will ultimately be whole, but it may not mean right now in this life.

The best way I know how to describe it is to say that the veil between this life and the blink that is the next is extremely thin, especially around death. Forgive me if it seems that I framed that too esoterically. I was thinking of Stephen at his stoning when the heavens opened (Acts 7:55). When we see a glimpse of a terminally ill person becoming whole and feel a confirmation in our spirit that is strong, we need to check to be sure we aren't being given a glimpse into eternity.

How do we check to see if God means a healing is for here or if He is making a statement about eternity? Ask the Holy Spirit for guidance about how to pray. It helps if we learn to be Spirit-led when we pray for others, and not just drug around by our emotions. While it is right to express our emotions in prayer, we need to be careful about using them as a filter to interpret spiritual data.

So often I have been guilty of praying from my emotions, from my vantage point outside of eternity. But I'm learning that, if all of this really is about Him, then shouldn't even sickness and death be about Him? If, in the grand scheme of things, God gets more glory by calling a child or elder "home," can I hold that against Him? And if in His plan, what seems unfair and painful actually brings Him glory I can't fathom, can I really pick up a gavel to play judge?

There are great examples that juxtapose our vantage point to God's in Scripture. Peering into how He gets glory from our lives is extremely helpful when answering the tough questions that will quite possibly emerge in this essential. For further reading that will get your blood pumping, check out *Cat & Dog Theology* by Bob Sjogren.

If you will train using the material here with sincerity and a willing heart, it will work. All the preliminary jitters, what ifs and questions will work themselves out, if you'll put yourself out there at 100%. If you're still not sure, then please know I've walked in your shoes. Relax. It's about Him, not you. He can handle it. Let the Holy Spirit lead you step by step.

I've seen some wild and crazy things as a result of children's audacity to believe! You will too, and if you're like me, you'll most likely need a dose of it for yourself. So, do you have the audacity to believe John 14:12 includes you and your children? If you do, jump in! If you don't, ask Him to cause you to acquire what you'll need. And remember, a little goes a long way; a dab'll do ya. Think mustard seeds transplanting mountains.

Got audacity? (No white mustache required.)

DISCOVERIES

When the Church releases children for ministry their audacity to believe reflects God's glory as they do some of the same works Jesus did.

When the work of Jesus through children is accepted, extraordinary things happen. At first it will grab a lot of attention, because it's not normal. Over time however, if children are encouraged to grow in this, the extraordinary becomes the new normal. It's not that the shiny wears off; it just becomes accepted practice for children to pray and for God to heal, deliver and answer. And that's a good thing.

Although there is no formula for answered prayers, there is a technique that can be used to train children to participate in the plans God has for the entire body of Christ.

Praying twice, or three times, for a problem is no problem for God, and does not necessarily reflect a lack of faith. In some situations, even Jesus touched people more than once to make them whole.

A note about pain: When praying for someone in pain, the first step may be to pray that the pain, a symptom of the problem, leave. Dissipating pain can bolster faith for complete healing.

IMPLEMENTATION: CHILDREN

The same Holy Spirit that fills adults, fills children—they do not get a "Holy Spirit Jr." version.

Since children will be doing the works of Jesus, relate stories to them of how He was moved with compassion for others and what that might have felt like. Tell stories of the miraculous things He did and how the miracles impacted other people. This will help prepare kids for how their prayers will be answered and what to expect.

Being able to "listen" for the voice of Jesus will be very important in developing this essential. Children's sensitivity to God's voice will allow them opportunities to obey.

Many times, we as teachers do not give training in this area because we are afraid God might not answer a child's prayer. We are concerned that we'll have to clean up God's mess, so to speak, if children are to work through disappointment in themselves or God. Understand that this teaching in Scripture is for all believers. And truth be told, God does not need us to worry about His reputation. Examine any barrier you may have about this, such as pride, fear, or unbelief. And, if in doubt, focus on the Word. Don't withhold information that may lead to someone's deliverance down the road.

Praying specifically for healing is important because it allows children and those who receive healing to know beyond a doubt that the prayer for healing was answered. It allows all parties involved to give glory to God.

Imagine specific praying as a "smart bomb" that can be used at precisely the right place at the right time. If praying specifically expands our faith, then praying in generalities shrinks it.

Do children need to be filled with the Holy Spirit to pray for the healing of others in Jesus' name? Not necessarily. Healing comes through the stripes Jesus took before His death, through the use of His name in prayer, and through faith. All New Testament examples point to the name being the key, not someone's level of spiritual fullness.

IMPLEMENTATION: ADULTS

It is normal for adults to hedge about the true nature of a physical problem with a child. Encourage adults to change this perception. They need to answer questions about their need for healing with honesty, giving information that will empower a child to be an informed intercessor.

A common prayer request by an adult might be for "pain in my body." Encourage adults to be more specific or not to be angered if a child presses for further information before praying. This simple adjustment in sharing the nature of a need builds trust and deepens relationships between adults and children in the assembly.

CREATIVE IDEAS

1. L.A.B.B. Method

This, to me, is one of the easiest methods to follow when praying for others. Be sure to train, not only teach this material. Let children practice on each other first, then on those who are sick and would like to be healed. The more children train in this area, the more equipped they are to exercise their faith and dominion as Spirit-filled believers.

Step One: Listen

There are three ways to listen for an opportunity to pray for someone's healing: (1) by someone asking to be prayed for (a child has to listen/pay attention), (2) by overhearing someone speak of a need for healing (hearing someone tell a friend about his/her ailment), and (3) by listening to the Holy Spirit as it leads (perhaps an impression or feeling that someone needs prayer).

Step Two: Ask

Children need to ask for permission before praying for anyone. Also, if they have been asked to pray for someone's healing, they may need to ask exactly what to pray for (back pain, cancer, blind eyes, etc.). This allows the child to pray on the spot, instead of waiting for a more "convenient" time to pray. It also engages the faith of the person asking for healing.

Step Three: Build Faith

This step is very important because it is the foundation of receiving the healing. How do children build faith? By relating a short testimony of how Jesus has answered a prayer for them or for someone they know.

After they have built faith, encourage children to ask this simple question: "Do you believe that when I pray for you, Jesus will hear me and heal you?" If they are answered with a bold "YES!" then they should proceed to pray. If not, they are to continue to build faith until they feel led by the Holy Spirit to begin praying. It's not a bad idea to confirm this by asking the question again, although it isn't exactly necessary. They are looking for a witness in their spirit to proceed with prayer.

Step Four: Be Bold

Bold praying is done in Jesus' name, using the word "NOW!" This is a point in prayer where people are to take authority over the ailment or situation causing pain. Doing this generates expectancy. Rather than praying for someone later, or "hoping God will help" the person at some point, using NOW! in the prayer shifts expectancy into the present moment.

When praying for someone, use a phrase like, "Right NOW! in the name of Jesus..." Put the phrase at the beginning of the prayer or towards the end. As children practice this, one or the other will feel more natural to them, and that is what you want. You want them to feel as comfortable and natural as possible.

2. Prayer Cloths

Use prayer cloths, anointed with oil by the children to give or send to someone who is in need of healing. After the cloth is anointed with oil, ask the children to lay hands on it or pass it from one to another, praying for the specific need.

This practice comes from the example of the apostle Paul in the New Testament, found in Acts 19:11-12: *"God gave Paul the power to do unusual miracles, so that even when handkerchiefs or cloths that had touched his skin were placed on sick people, they were healed of their diseases, and any evil spirits within them came out".*

To modernize this practice further, use Band-Aids; kids especially like the ones with characters on them. Also, kiddie-looking pieces of cloth small enough to fit in a wallet work great and are keepsakes after healing takes place.

You'll find oil can be a little messy for children to handle, so, you may want to take advantage of a kid-friendly dispenser available from kidsprayer.com. A small oil bottle, the size of a lip balm tube, uses a roller ball to dispense the oil in small amounts. There are also "Prayer for Healing" kits available for purchase to jump-start your efforts.

3. Corporate Church Services

Include children in ministry time, allowing them to lay hands on the sick along with ministry leaders of the congregation.

4. Healing line

Instruct children to form a healing line in a children's service or an adult service, and ask those with needs for healing to come through the line in groups by topic of prayer need. For example, all those with back pain, come through the line together. Perhaps then you may ask all those with headaches to come through the line. This way the children will know how to specifically target their prayers to the needs.

STORIES

Each time I have taught the L.A.B.B. Method to children or adults, God has provided a live demonstration of His power. <u>Do</u> try this at home!

1. Denver, Colorado

A lady was healed of a bone infection when a girl practiced using the L.A.B.B. Method for the first time.

2. Bentley, Louisiana

The pastor's wife suffered from severe pain in one of her heels until three girls prayed for her.

3. Bridgeton, Missouri

One of the class teachers was healed of a severe ear infection, receiving her hearing after kids prayed and then commanded, "Ears hear, in Jesus' name!" This really works!

4. Ghana, East Africa

A lady with a fractured knee was healed when kids who had been listening in on an adult training session used the L.A.B.B. Method to pray for her. She was so excited that she came to the adult session the next day to share her testimony and lead in worship.

5. Honduran KP Miracle

Sahari, a Sunday school teacher from Honduras, determined in her heart to train children in her church to pray after attending a regional KP emphasis training seminar. Little did she know that this decision would literally save her life.

One day Sahari became very ill and was given an injection of the wrong medication. This caused bleeding in her brain and the complete loss of her memory. At the point when doctors had given her less than three hours to live, something happened. One of her ten-year-old Sunday school students arrived to pray for her. And that changed everything.

Sulimar, her student, had run to the hospital, laid her hands on her teacher's head and asked the Lord not to take her teacher yet because she knew there was so much more to learn from her. Soon Sahari's bleeding stopped and, over time, her memory was restored.

6. Prayer Cloth

Lois' hand began to swell for no reason. Within minutes she could not use her hand at all. I had a kids prayer cloth with me that had a general prayer prayed over it by a group of kids. The moment I gave the cloth to Lois, she wedged it between her fingers. In less than thirty minutes, the swelling had lessened greatly and she could use her hand. She kept the cloth in place and the swelling went completely away.

Not long after, Jimmy, her husband, was diagnosed with throat cancer. They requested that my kids prayer group send an anointed prayer cloth. A while after being declared cancer free, he showed me how he'd kept the cloth in his wallet as a reminder of God's goodness.

7. Band-Aid Prayer

One evening before church, Eric called his children down to the basement to ask them to pray for him because he wasn't feeling well. After they prayed, they went back upstairs to finish getting ready for church. A few minutes later, Jared, his nine-year-old, came back downstairs with a Band-Aid in his hand.

Jared told his dad he felt to pray again and give him a Band-Aid. He asked where his dad was hurting, prayed briefly, then placed the Band-Aid on his dad's shirt over the spot. He turned around and went back upstairs. Within a few minutes Eric realized he was fine and shared the news with his kids on the way to church.

8. Like Daughters, Like Mother

Mary-Jo, a mother of girls who were involved in kids prayer training, injured her knee at work. By the time she made it back to her desk, she was in a lot of pain. She decided to do what her girls would have done had they been there. She put her hand on her knee and prayed a simple prayer, just like her girls. Within five minutes her knee was back to normal.

9. One Thing Leads To Another

A young girl had just finished using the L.A.B.B. Method to pray for a missionary to Honduras, in front of a crowd of curious Sunday school teachers. Though the training seminar was for adults, this girl wasn't afraid to try what she had overheard. As a result of praying a few times for 100% of the pain to go, the missionary was able to raise her arm, pain free, which was  something she had not been able to do for months.

This small act of obedience and faith led to many miracles. One in particular, demonstrates what being led by the Holy Spirit looks like.

As faith shot through the congregation, with a simple invitation, people flocked to the front for prayer. As the host missionary moved with her camera through the crowd to document this special move of God, she noticed a little lady hunched over the steps praying. So intent on getting great pictures to share with others, she nearly stepped over the lady, but stopped suddenly when the thought crossed her mind, "This lady must need something. I'll just lay my hand on her as I walk by." *This was a prompt by the Holy Spirit.*

Missionary Lynne held her camera in one hand and, putting her other hand lightly on the lady's back and prayed, "Lord, take care of this lady's need in Jesus' name." After this, she proceeded up the steps and went on to take pictures of the miracles happening all around her. It was so exciting!

The next morning, this little lady gave her testimony. She had traveled two days, standing up on a bus, in excruciating pain to get to the meeting. Until the previous night, she had suffered 17 years with back pain and needed to walk with a cane. As she prayed on those steps, she told God, "If someone would lay their hand on me, I know I'll be healed."

When Lynn rested her hand lightly on this lady's back, the lady felt the deviated disk that had caused her pain for so many years, pop back into place. After that, she realized she was pain free. That night, though her bed was a piece of cardboard on a hard cement floor, she woke up without any pain.

What a difference a little girl's prayer made on a missionary and a crowd of Sunday school teachers. What a difference that little lady's honest cry to God made. What a difference a simple but Spirit-led prayer made.

We never know how our obedience fits into the larger plans of God. The fact that you know about these events proves that He had something bigger in mind all along. God can use anyone, even you. Just listen and obey.

Chapter 7: ARMOR

Clearheaded and Protected

CORE VALUE –I Thessalonians 5:4-8

But you aren't in the dark about these things, dear brothers and sisters, and you won't be surprised when the day of the Lord comes like a thief. [b] For you are all children of the light and of the day; we don't belong to darkness and night. So be on your guard, not asleep like the others. Stay alert and be clearheaded. Night is the time when people sleep and drinkers get drunk. But let us who live in the light be clearheaded, protected by the armor of faith and love, and wearing as our helmet the confidence of our salvation.

Surprised? You were expecting maybe Ephesians 6 for this core value? I'll admit it's what I used the first time. However, this time I hit a snag.

I understand that praying my spiritual armor on daily serves as a reminder of the protection and weapons I have at my disposal. However, I've always wondered, if I put the armor on through prayer, at which point does it fall off each day? When I have a bad thought or behavior? When I sleep? If it doesn't come off, why do I have to pray it on again the next day? Am I supposed to take it off? And, what I really want to know is, is it possible for me to learn to pray it on so well that it will stay on forever? What happens if I forget to pray it on? Why is it I usually remember to pray it on during a time of crisis and stress in my life? See what I mean? I hit a snag.

If I've entertained these questions, you can be pretty sure some of your kids will wonder the same things and more.

You know what kind of armor I envision the Body having? Something akin to Transformers*. Spiritual armor that is integrated into my spirit and goes into action when it's needed. This is the image I've been working from for quite some time, not that of a Roman soldier. The cool thing about a Transformer-type armor is it's not just individually applicable, but collectively as well. And, this is not a kind of armor one puts on, it's a kind of armor one is…or becomes.

After the initial giving of information and getting children to realize that they need protection from the enemy of their soul, how do we get them to apply it? Because what they need is to apply it in such a way that the armor becomes a part of them spiritually, as much a part of them spiritually as their flesh is a part of them physically.

I think this is the real point, getting from spirit wrapped in flesh to spirit protected by spiritual armor, wrapped in flesh. This is where our real efforts need to focus and 1 Thessalonians 5:4-8 gives an idea of what being decked in spiritual armor looks like. It looks like a Body that's clearheaded and protected.

Training children to know and understand the content of Ephesians 6 is vital in grounding them and educating them on the way things really are, spiritually speaking. We need to do this, but we can't stop there. Praying on spiritual armor isn't enough. Children need to learn how to live in the light and to be on their guard. Thankfully for them, this is what the other six essentials will help them do.

As part of teaching Ephesians 6 content, it is of growing importance that our children understand they should pay attention to their relationships. Building good relationships will keep them from having enemies, outside of the one, mortal enemy of us all. These days, relationships of every kind are being challenged and in the days to come the challenges will only increase. If the enemy can keep us fighting among ourselves, holding grudges, and living in unforgiveness, then the Body of Christ is far from clearheaded and it is certainly unprotected.

This is where prayer comes in. Prayer, like in the six essentials previously explored, moves us from ritual to amalgamation, becoming one with Christ. And when we are one with Him, being wrapped in spiritual armor is a much more natural and organic process than a mechanical one. The way Paul described it, as people walking in light we put on Christ (Romans 13:13-14) and are then able to choose not to do evil.

Interesting. Paul wrote to one group in Ephesus to put on the whole armor of God. To another group, the Romans, he wrote to put on Christ. To those in Galatia, he said they put on Christ at baptism. And to the group in Thessalonica, he gave advice to wear a breastplate and helmet. Notice how Paul addressed the needs of different groups by giving them applicable analogies? He was shooting for an end result, not a systematic approach.

I'm curious. Which are you more like? Ephesians, Romans, Galatians or Thessalonians? As a routine, what would you rather do? Put on Christ and be empowered, or put on pieces of spiritual equipment? They produce the same result, but the thought process is much different. With one, humans do the heavy lifting of remembering and applying; with the other, it's Christ who does the work. For me, as I aim to keep my life about Christ, the first option suits me better. You may prefer something else and that's okay.

As you go through this material, the goal is the outcome, not so much a standardized methodology. Getting your children to be clearheaded and protected may mean putting on heaps of armor (Ephesians), accepting the work of Christ's death (Galatians), aligning with Christ (Romans), or possibly focusing on faith, love and believing (Thessalonians). Getting to the outcome may mean walking through each of Paul's analogies to protectively clothe as many children in your care as possible.

As I wrote in Chapter 1, I believe that we are living in the last days, a time just prior to Christ's return. 1 Thessalonians 5:3 has an interesting statement by Paul that bears pointing out. He wrote that we, who are children of the light, will *not* be caught by surprise when Christ returns. He also admonishes us to be alert and clearheaded.

If ever there was a time to heed this advice, it is now. Things we may have been taught in the past need to be double-checked for integrity. Make sure you have confidence in your salvation.

There is a shaking coming that would like to knock the helmet of "the confidence of our salvation" off of our collective head. As a global Body of Christ, we cannot afford to lose faith, love or confidence in our salvation. Hang onto these things, fight for them, nurture them and protect them in the Body with all your soul.

Put on Christ. Be transformed. Stay clearheaded and protected.

*Transformers: unique machines that transform from common mechanical objects to fighting robots; they can fight individually or join up collectively.

DISCOVERIES: Prayer Giftings

Understanding the concept of prayer giftings is helpful in applying the use of spiritual armor. In simple terms, a prayer gifting is the way a person is comfortable operating in prayer, in line with their personality. We may not fight flesh and blood, but our enemy isn't beyond using flesh and blood to inflict harm to us spiritually. For more detailed information see this topic in the bonus material.

A person's spiritual armor is designed to protect any weakness in their personality and giftings. Because we are not all the same and since we all have different jobs within the Body, it follows that we need protection according to these variances. It's universal that we need protection; how that protection is applied is unique to each person. Thanks to Paul and the Holy Spirit, we have an idea of the basic areas that we need to make sure are covered well.

Let's work through an example. If someone is sensitive to God, it's most likely that they are also sensitive to others, and may get their feelings hurt easily. Which piece of armor would be important to augment and protect this gift? Shoes? A belt? Most likely, the breastplate, as it covers the area of a person's heart. As one applies the truth the breastplate holds, the protection becomes a part of them to the point that in the future, their feelings are protected, keeping sensitivity intact.

DISCOVERIES

Don't expect all children to sound alike when they pray, and certainly don't expect them to sound like adults.

Nurture children to discover their giftings and help make a place for those gifts in the local church. The sooner a child's gifts are identified, the sooner he can begin using them.

Become familiar with the "Body of Christ", Romans 12:5-8, and gifts from the Holy Spirit, 1 Corinthians 12:4-11.

Use imagery that reflects real world applications when talking about protection. Eg: Soldier, Fireman, and Policeman

The small picture is: we need to protect ourselves spiritually from spiritual attacks. The big picture is: we collectively make up one Body of Christ, therefore we need to protect that Body by protecting ourselves and the gifts God has placed in His Body on earth.

IMPLEMENTATION

Help children identify their gifts at early ages (as early as preschool some indicators will be evident). Observations by parents and ministry leaders as well as specialized tests can help determine these gifts. Tests such as the DISC test can be simplified and given to primary students. There are a few stewardship tests out there, but most of them are not intended for children.

Although abilities and interests are in a state of flux as a child develops, patterns will be evident. Once gifts are identified, or you understand a child's predisposition to certain things, such as missions, prophesy, dreams/visions, teaching, and mercy to name a few, allow or give him opportunities to exercise his gifts in private and public/corporate settings.

Explain the truths of the pieces of armor in Ephesians 6 often. Make sure children understand how their spirit can be protected. As you go along, help children apply these truths—pray the truths into their lives—as a means of putting the armor on.

Here is something subtle to try when putting Jesus first in prayer. Try replacing the idea of needing "help" with the idea of asking God to "cause" something. Asking God to help me puts me in control. Asking Him to cause something demonstrates my dependency on Him. It helps keep us from a "Genie in the bottle mentality."

Example: Jesus, help me pass the test.

      Jesus, cause me to study well to pass the test.

Example: Jesus, help me not to yell at my sister.

      a. Jesus, cause my sister to love me more so I won't lose my temper with her as much.

      b. Jesus, cause me to love my sister more so I won't yell at her.

      c. Jesus, cause me to show love to my sister no matter what.

CREATIVE IDEAS

1. Listen and Pay Attention

Listen to children as they share with you what the Holy Spirit puts on their hearts. These topics will become threads through their development that will let you know their giftings and "burdens" for others. These gifts need to be protected to be useful long-term.

2. Build Awareness Through Prayer Activity

To help build awareness, get children to commit to praying on the armor daily for a period of time (a week, a month). A "Getting-ready-to-leave-the-house" routine may serve as a helpful daily reminder. These are just starter ideas, not a model to follow.

      Helmet While combing hair pray, *"Protect my mind from the taunting of the enemy. My thoughts determine who I am and how I act. Keep it pure!"*

      Breastplate While putting on shirt, blouse or dress pray, *"Protect my heart and my spirit. My feelings are protected behind this barrier, so help them not to be* *so easily hurt by others. My spiritual "ears" are also protected by this piece, so help me keep my sensitivity to You all day long."*

Belt While putting on pants, skirt or belt pray, *"Let me be full of the truth, which includes always telling the truth. Don't let me associate with liars or allow me to cheat in relationships, tests, or anything else."*

Shield When picking up a backpack, *"Cause my faith to be strong to stop the fiery weapons of the enemy. I know the enemy hates me, but I need to remember that You love me and nothing I can ever do will change that! Cause me be someone who builds up faith in myself and others."*

Shoes When putting on shoes, *"Give me peace by remembering how You came to save us all. I must use my feet to carry Your "good news" to others who are so full of the effects of darkness. I do not need to be afraid!"*

Sword When brushing teeth or some other activity, *"I need to use Your Word as my weapon against any trick of the enemy. Help me put more of Your Word in me so I can be prepared. Your Word is strong, powerful, and quicker than anything, slicing to bits anything that is not of You."*

3. Open Understanding

Explain the idea of prayer giftings and spiritual gifts in general. Explain and give visual examples of how modern day soldiers, firemen, policemen, etc., use protection to help them do their jobs. Spend time contrasting and comparing various kinds of armor or protective gear.

Note how soldiers, firemen, and policemen all wear the same parts of armor to protect their head, chest, and feet. And they each have a "weapon" of some kind. However, because their jobs are different, they are protected from and fight different elements (eg: bullets, fire) in different ways. **Brainstorm** to identify different giftings and the special armor each one needs.

STORIES

1. Benton, Louisiana

After giving information about the armor of God and how if we could see each other spiritually we might see different armor, I asked children to sit quietly, asking God to show them what their armor looked like. After less than two minutes, a young boy shared this insight with our group.

His armor made him look like a baseball player at bat. He explained, "the batting helmet protects my head, the bat is my weapon, the kneepads and shin guard are my shields (along with that other protective piece which caused a ripple of laughter), and the cleats are my special shoes." When someone asked him why a baseball player, he responded, "Because, I'm a team player."

2. Mimi's Lesson

Following is a great example to show a few different ways people might approach the same situation and how it might reveal the way they pray. *(Adapted with permission from Thetus Tenney.)*

On the way to prayer meeting one night, I prepared a cake to share with the group afterwards. I was running late when I arrived, so from the driver's side I quickly grabbed the cake from the passenger seat and as I was closing the door behind me, I dropped the cake. To the ground. A few people came running...

Mercy gift – "Oh my goodness! You poor thing. Here, let me help you pick this up. Here, use these wet wipes." (Prays with empathy and perhaps with a lot of tears.)

Prophetic gift – "Wow! When I saw you getting out of the car, I just knew you were going to drop the cake." (Prays in a way that is more about the message, than the person.)

Organizational gift – "I'm running late too. I'll send someone back out here to help." (Prays with a list and or on a set schedule.)

Know-it-all gift – "Next time take your cake out from the passenger side, not the driver's side. You wouldn't want to waste another cake." (Prays as if giving advice to God.) *There is some debate as to whether or not this is actually a "gift."*

Chapter 8: MINISTRY

All For God's Glory

Passing of the Keys

As children grow spiritually, they *will use* what they learn. How does the Body of Christ respond to this infusion of energy, lack of experience, and need for opportunity? Often, they respond by shutting it down. Adults in church leadership are often afraid children who minister will become arrogant and difficult to manage. What they don't understand is that your efforts to train children to respond to their hunger for God's glory actually protects them from inflated egos.

When children who minister are treated as normal, and not like some special freak of nature, ministry comes naturally. And believe me, kids keep each other in line, especially if someone gets too big for his britches. Children have no qualms about helping someone keep their head and they can be brutally honest and transparent with each other if such an environment is nurtured properly. Although this level of honesty is something the vast majority of adults struggle with, children can handle it.

So, how do you get adults to understand a desire to put God's glory ahead of everything else? Unless you are a leader or a pastor, it may prove difficult to influence elders and parents to change their thinking about children. For many, children are still to be seen and not heard. Many are offended by spiritual "play," and parents are often distracted from noticing spiritual progress due to busy lives and responsibilities.

External Measures

You can try external measures. What's an external measure? Something generated outside of a person's emotions, providing information by way of report or example.

External measures may include such activities as sending home fliers or posting a note in the bulletin about what God is doing. You may even be able to schedule a few special events or get children in front of the congregation for a prayer activity, such as an offering prayer or opening prayer before service.

However, if these external measures don't work, or you want to try something else first, an internal measure may be what you're looking for.

Internal Measures

An internal measure is something generated from the inside, from the spirit of those you are seeking to influence; be it elders, parents or leaders. I am not suggesting manipulation, but I am suggesting providing an opportunity for elders, parents, and leaders to become personally invested in the ministries and lives of children in the local church. It's hard to ignore something you've invested in isn't it?

In addition to intergenerational prayer meetings and kids prayer show and tell, I have used an internal measure on several occasions and it has proven to be a useful and versatile tool. We commonly use this tool at events like graduations, weddings, and award distribution. In simple terms, we have a ceremony. Following is the back-story on where the idea came from, and ways to make modifications to fit a particular need.

Passing of the Keys: Breakthrough Resistance

A few years into traveling around holding Kids Prayer training meetings, I met very strong resistance at a particular church and it took me a bit by surprise. In every case up to that point, those who invited me were ready for the material and hungry for change. Though the pastor and Sunday school teachers were all for developing children in prayer, some of the elders were offended by some of the KP worship ideas and the concept of children ministering to elders.

On the night before our last day together, I remembered packing an oversized set of skeleton keys. At the time I didn't know why I had thrown them into my bag, but the Holy Spirit dropped an idea into my mind that was genius.

The next morning, as children worshipped freely (and a few elders walked out), I was prompted by the Holy Spirit to ask the leadership who the "pillars" of prayer in the church were. An elderly couple was pointed out to me, and that was all the confirmation I needed. I was set. Nervous, but set.

When the pulpit was turned over to me, I did my usual thing. I greeted the congregation and cast a vision for kids prayer using all the tools in my kit: videos, pictures and stories. Now it was time for those keys.

I showed the keys to the congregation and thanked them for keeping the keys to revival and prayer safe all these years. I went on to explain that, just as it is important for kids to learn responsibility at home, it is important for them to learn spiritual responsibility too. It was time for children to help with the praying and evangelizing. It was time for children to use their energies to bring God glory, but they didn't have access to the keys for these things because they were so carefully guarded.

By this time, all eyes were on those keys as I absentmindedly waved them around. Then, the Holy Spirit reminded me to call on the elderly couple pointed out to me earlier. I asked them to come to the front and accept the keys from me as a representation of all their years of faithful service. They came, hankies in hand and stood facing the congregation.

Next, I asked for the children who wanted to use the keys like this couple to come and stand, facing them. I discouraged any child from coming who wasn't interested in using the keys of prayer and revival; most of them came forward. At this point, I saw a few other hankies dabbing eyes here and there in the congregation.

I asked one little girl to accept the keys for everyone else. Then, I asked the elders to take turns praying the keys from their lives into the lives of the children before them. As soon as they finished praying, that little girl grabbed the microphone and prayed a prayer of thanks to God that somebody FINALLY shared the keys with them. Then she added, "and help us kids share the keys with other littler kids too."

In that moment, the Holy Spirit had just the atmosphere He wanted. I moved out of the way after giving simple instructions for any adult who wanted to be blessed or prayed for by children to step into the aisle. The Holy Spirit began melting hearts as children ministered freely. The resistance we'd felt through our training evaporated.

Passing of the Keys: Build Faith

On another occasion, the situation was different in that children so highly regarded their leaders that they couldn't believe God would use children like themselves to bring Him glory. So, I pulled out a set of keys and did a similar ceremony, but this time Sunday school teachers released their giftings and anointings through prayer over those children. Although no one is mystically changed by what others say over them, people are changed by what they choose to believe; and children are people too.

As children heard teachers investing in them with their own ears they began to believe that God really was giving them training to do the works of Jesus. He really would receive glory from their lives and efforts as they listened and followed Him.

Upon accepting the challenge their teachers made and upon believing what their teachers prayed, ministry broke out among children, then turned into ministry by children to adults. It was the breakthrough needed to dispel unbelief.

They knew it was time to move from ministry to children to ministry by children.

Passing the Keys: Down the Chain of Command

It was the chance of a lifetime to travel with a fellow children's minister to Ghana, West Africa, for a teacher training seminar and children's crusade. Once we arrived, I shared the idea with the missionary of doing a "key ceremony" at the end of the training. Not only was the idea accepted, the missionary arranged for each attendee to receive a blank key on a ribbon that could be worn around the neck as a reminder of the ceremony.

By the end of the training seminar, I'd realized that many of the national leaders were in attendance. Another way to put that last sentence is, the Holy Spirit called to my attention that many of the national leaders were in attendance. Though I'd first thought to pass the keys from missionaries to Sunday school teachers, the

Holy Spirit checked me and sent me down a slightly different chain of command.

When it was time, I called the national leaders forward and solicited one to pray, giving a blessing to use the 7 Essentials as keys in the local church. Next, I called pastors forward who were willing to receive the keys through prayer.

Once the pastors had accepted the keys from their leaders, I called the Sunday school teachers and other leaders forward who were willing to use the keys their pastors would pray over them. A pastor prayed a mighty prayer, then a teacher prayed the final prayer of thanksgiving for the authority to use keys passed down from national leaders. I learned later that this was a rather big deal for them.

In the mad scramble to get a ceremonial key to take home, I noticed that faces were aglow. God had done it again.

Ministry By Children

Well, you've been reading long enough, don't you think? Following are pictures to help illustrate what ministry by children looks like. Being a part of this endeavor has changed my life and brought much glory to God. May you see more than just children in these pictures; may you see Him through them.

All for His glory!

Ministering in a nursing home. Children prayed for needs
and gave handmade gifts to each attendee.

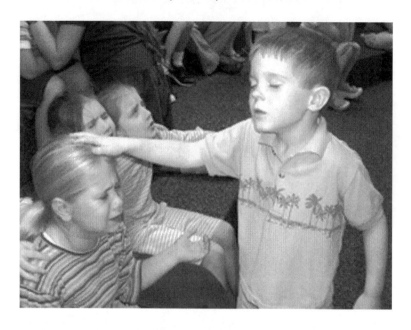

Laying hands on others is okay.
This is Tyler's favorite way to pray.

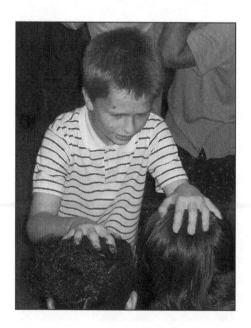

Above: This girl's grandmother was healed of a bone infection after a child used the L.A.B.B. Method.
Below: Eunice prays the Word as the opening prayer of a national conference in Guatemala.

Praying for pastors is encouraged. Above: This pastor was surprised at the intensity of prayer and the effective approach children used to ask him how he wanted them to pray. Below: This pastor is accustomed to children gathering around him before service to pray.

Children pray for their "Big Church" worship leader before service.

A child in China prays for her parents during a ministry time.

An outgrowth of kids prayer…
Above: Teaching children in Bangladesh.
Below: Visiting an orphanage in Guatemala.

Kids prayer raises up leaders and helps children
put their talents where their prayers are.
Above: Saturday School of Prayer Leadership Team
Below: Preparing shoe boxes for Operation Christmas Child

PART TWO

BONUS MATERIAL

Part Two Introduction

When I was first drawn to leading children in prayer, I stumbled on a historical element that surprised me. Dating back several hundred years, when great revivals broke out children were some of the first to respond.

In America during the 1700's children were some of the first to respond to the preaching of Jonathan Edwards; their lives radically changed.

In Scotland, during the great revival in the late 1800's, children were some of the first to spark the roaring flames that burned for many years.

In the early 1900's children were again right in the middle of revival. This time in Los Angeles, during the Azuza Street Revival that birthed the Pentecostal movement. In the late 1900's at the Brownsville Revival in Pensacola, Florida, children were again in the thick of it.

It surprised me to discover some of the details about children in these revivals because it didn't seem to have much impact on the way children were subsequently taught about God. Over and over again adults commenting on children's involvement were surprised.

It would seem to me teachers would have been interested to uncover and dissect what it was about these moves of God that appealed to children. Perhaps some did. Had it caught on, it would have allowed teachers to move away from a traditional teaching approach to a training and ministry solution. One that would support children in a more deliberate course toward spiritual development.

Perhaps the reason they didn't is because that time is now. Could it be it's our turn as teachers and trainers to do things differently? I can't escape thinking of how much glory God would get from such a change. Maybe, just maybe kids prayer is an important step in making that change.

In the last decade, the idea of training kids to operate in a spiritual capacity has steadily gained ground, extending beyond physical and spiritual borders. Yes, this message has made it into many countries, even closed ones, and has crossed denominational lines. Information concerning the piece that is Kids Prayer (KP) has never been more in demand. Its simplicity and relevancy defies decline, flourishing even in hard times. And now, here you are. For some of you, here you are...again. I hope this is what you've been looking for, "The 7 Essentials 2.0."

Since this handbook sold its first copy, much of the world has moved from paperbacks to e-readers, from basic cell phones to smart ones, and from hard cash to plastic. A lot has changed it seems, but the seven original core values haven't. The methods of application, however, continue to evolve with each passing year and I hope it continues. Methods and information we knew nothing of a few years ago are emerging. Concepts that took time to plow, plant and grow in the past are now the standard. New understandings are redistributing parts of the initial framework, but the core is still there.

Looking back, if I were to gauge which part of this handbook was used most during the previous edition, it would be the chapters on "Worship" and "Kingdom Praying." In general, our focus was primarily on the harvest, our motivation was for souls. This served as a giant leap away from a "Sunday school" model, which is great for passing on information, but lacks in providing space to experience God. Those who have taken the leap are in many cases successfully training children to see beyond themselves, to live for His glory.

While this emphasis is still desperately needed, there is a growing need to raise up believers who know who they are in Jesus, can hear Him speak clearly and are willing to do what He asks when He asks. Though the handbook is designed specifically to help you enable believers who happen to be children, the core values and bonus material are for anyone.

Looking forward, in the months and years ahead, I am certain the chapter on "Listening," bumped up a few chapters from the previous edition, will rise in importance and practice. In fact, I see indicators that it's already begun. May our focus primarily be on hearing God personally. Our motivation? Bringing Him, and only Him, glory. May any other motivation be measured against that of His glory and be found wanting.

For this season, I sense the other six essentials will work seamlessly once "listening" is in place. Can you imagine what 6-8 years of KP training with a focus on bringing God glory will bring? Much glory to the One who deserves it all. If the harvest is plentiful, He gets the glory. If a need is met, He gets glory. If someone is healed, He gets glory. If someone is able to stand against the enemy, God gets glory. Let Him revel in it.

For those who have doubts. At a children's ministry equipping conference in 2003, one of the main points driven home was, "Children are hungry for the supernatural." At the time, I took a look around me to see if the statement fit the group I ministered to. As I did so, I noticed the newest batch of TV shows was touting supernatural content and my kids were familiar with it. Further examination revealed a culture filled with mystical creatures in cartoons and games. Again, my kids were right in the middle of it all.

The Harry Potter craze was in high gear and the Twilight phenomenon was getting started, and yes, some of my kids couldn't wait for the next book to come out. When I put it all together, I realized the hunger was stronger than anything my childhood memories could excuse. "I Dream of Jeannie," "Bewitched," and "Wonder Woman," were like doorways of curiosity and imagination to my generation that opened up darker places for those behind us. Things had changed.

To be honest, in those days I wasn't sure if the Jesus I could share would be "supernatural enough" for my kids. Turing water into wine was old school. Waking on water? Really? How about something 21st century? I didn't think I could present Him in such a way that He could compete. It was about that time I met Miss Sue, a mom hungry for a move of God in her children who evolved into a kids prayer leader. She explained it wasn't my job to paint Jesus in a certain light, but I was to simply bring my kids to Him and let Him do the talking. That released a pressure valve in me and marginalized my hereditary performance gene. I began to realize I wasn't responsible to make anything happen, only facilitate in a journey.

So, as you take a look around you, perhaps even in your own home, you'll realize we're inundated with supernatural content that is feeding a generation in place of the Bread of Life. When your doubts rise about whether or not you're cut out to answer this call to train children hungry for the supernatural, let me be your "Miss Sue" when I say, take your children to Him and let Him do the talking. You will need to check out the path first, which is the reason I'm writing this bonus material. As you become familiar with the path, I hope you'll discover its delights. And I hope you discover just how much Jesus is delighted in you.

Speaking of delight, I believe I've discovered a key that will explain clearly how you can re-engineer a sagging KP structure, or build a strong one from scratch. It will require a move away from traditional thinking about the "discipline of prayer," and into a place of "delight in prayer." Although there is surely a place for discipline, surprisingly it doesn't necessarily have to come first. KP's staying power has much more to do with the word "delight" than it does "discipline."

Think about it for a moment. What happens when a child is forced to take up an activity he doesn't enjoy? He quits, doesn't put as much effort into it, or loses heart. Why would we expect it to be different spiritually? Coaching your group to be delighted as they do spiritual growth work, i.e. KP related activities or routines, is necessary and actually follows precedent in Scripture. I can't wait to unpack for you some of what I've learned personally in this area. It's been quite a journey.

So...go for it! For some of you, you are ready to begin at square one. For others, you're being nudged to bring on your A-game...again. The truths in these core essentials, born in revival fires through the past three hundred years, will work well alongside methods and information uncovered in this century.

For every decision along the way, may you hear His voice clearly. For every dark or confusing moment, "LET THERE BE LIGHT!"

Chapter 9: GOD DELIGHTS IN HIS CHILDREN

God inhabits praise, dwells in the heavens, exists outside of time, and delights in me…always. That's a fact, not a theory or a wish. Now, read that first sentence aloud like you mean it. Could you? If you've mostly been taught a performance-based version of Christianity, then no doubt you've had some trouble accepting this truth: God delights in me. He not only loves me, but He gets a kick out of me.

A Little Squirrelly

Acceptance is a funny thing. We accept salvation through what Christ did on the cross. No problem. We accept "the way things are," 90% of the time. No biggie. We even accept responsibility for things beyond our control. Who's counting? But we struggle accepting the truth of God's delight in us, His children. Strike that. Actually, we believe he delights in "us" collectively, but when it gets personal, we get squirrelly.

A two-year-old taught me my first lesson about "squirrelly." I tried my best to give Jordan a little treat, but he wouldn't take it from me. I could tell he wanted it, but he wouldn't participate in my plan to provide him with a sugar rush. Even when his twin brother, Morgan grabbed what I offered, Jordan refused and pretended to ignore me. Jordan was, in the words of his father, a little squirrelly at that age.

His dad suggested I set the treat on the edge of the counter where Jordan could reach it when he thought no one was looking. So, I

131

placed the treat, and then hid around the corner to see how long it would take Jordan to make his move. It wasn't long until his fingers closed around the treat I left for him.

Sometimes we get squirrelly too when God tries to offer us His unabashed delight. We want to delight Him desperately, but we are more willing to accept it if He will leave it for us to take on our own terms. Too many of us believe we should earn God's delight, but that is an "Old School" way of thinking.

This is where the teachings of the two Testaments collide. Law and grace are on unequal footing when it comes to explaining God's delight in us. In the Old Testament, a law-based system, God's delight in His people was contingent on their following *every* law and commandment. That's what I call a triple whammy; having to earn salvation and delight with a perfect score. I'd also call it an impossible dream.

The good news is in the New Testament the paradigm shifts (Hebrews 8:9). When I am filled with the Holy Spirit, I know my salvation issue is settled through Christ's work on the cross; a shift from law to grace. My delight issue is settled when I realize God delights in Himself. Why is that important to realize? Because when He puts His spirit in me, He sees Himself in me. When He sees Himself in me, He is delighted in me. Now that's grace that's amazing!

God Delights In Himself

How do I know God delights in Himself? Through Scripture. Although I must say, the first time someone showed me how God is delighted in Himself and how He brings glory to Himself it was a bit of a surprise.

Let's take a look at just a few of those Scriptures.

1. *"The Lord does whatever pleases him throughout all heaven and earth, and on the seas and in their depths"* (Psalm 135:6).

2. *"I am God and there is no other; I am God and there is none like me, declaring the end from the beginning and from ancient times things not yet undone, saying, 'My counsel shall stand, and I will accomplish all my pleasure"* (Isaiah 46:9-10).

Additionally, I get a clue about how God is pleased with Himself through the life of Jesus.

An Inkling Through Jesus

I get an inkling of God's delight in me best through the New Testament, and more clearly through Jesus. When I see the way Jesus delighted in doing the will of the Father on earth, and how it elicited a response of delight from the Father, I get it. As I delight in God, He delights in me. Nothing much in the Old Testament shows me this. I don't see clearly how to delight in God and I don't see evidence that He delighted much before the cross. I do see how much He ached for it but due to the nature of the law, He didn't get much of a shot at it.

Don't take me wrong, I love the Old Testament and all it offers believers today, but in the area of delight, it is somewhat difficult to apply. The New Testament, on the other hand, gives me examples of what God's delight looks like through the life of Jesus. Take a peek at God's delight through the Message Bible.

*"The moment Jesus came up out of the baptismal waters, the skies opened up and he saw God's Spirit—it looked like a dove—descending and landing on him. And along with the Spirit, a voice: "This is my Son, chosen and marked by my love, **delight** of my life"* (Matthew 3:16-17, MSG).

*"Look well at my handpicked servant; I love him so much, take such **delight** in him. I've placed my Spirit on him"* (Matthew 12:17-19, MSG).

*"While he was going on like this, babbling, a light-radiant cloud enveloped them, and sounding from deep in the cloud a voice: "This is my Son, marked by my love, focus of my **delight**. Listen to him"* (Matthew 17:5, MSG).

When I make my life about God, and not myself, my family, my religion or my denomination, I will be His delight, and He will be mine. Substituting anything else will be my headache or my disappointment.

Believable

Now we're getting warmer. Understanding God's delight through the life of Jesus leads me in a path away from myself. Experiencing God's delight comes when I understand all this is not about me, or us, rather it's all about Him. It's not about my performance, but about His faithfulness to Himself (2 Timothy 2:13). He isn't pinning His eternal happiness on me, or those I train. He pins His eternal happiness on Himself. Whew! What a relief.

I don't know about you, but for me, knowing God delights in Himself, makes it easier for me to believe He delights in me too. If

I am a joint heir with Christ, am I not also the focus of God's delight? If God has placed His Holy Spirit in me, it stands to reason He can take delight from my existence, because HE is in me...and He delights Himself.

For me, one of the biggest obstacles to gripping this bit of grace was the feeling that, there was nothing delightful about me. Sin does that to people. My "Mirror-Mirror-On-The-Wall", said one thing and the mirror of the Word said something else. Either I was worse than an ogre and as boring as a plain bowl of oatmeal, or it was a lie.

As I searched the Word, the ultimate mirror, there was a great clash between what the Word said about me and what I believed about myself. I couldn't go on with a double mind so I had to choose which voice to believe; I still do. You can guess which one I chose. I didn't want to live my like a swamp dwelling creature.

Feeling better about myself wasn't the key to getting a grip on grace, but it was a start. Take a look at the next statement. There's nothing delightful about *me*. See what just happened? In that frame of mind, I made God's delight about myself. When I consciously live to make life about Him, I may make a similar statement, but it would sound more like, "There's not much delightful about me, except for Him." See the faith in that? That faith plants a little seed of hope in my spirit that grows into a knowing.

As I learn to recognize and know God is in me, I learn to recognize and know He is delighted with me. Furthermore, recognizing this makes me delighted with Him. In my delight, subsequent works, worship, obedience, sacrifice, you name it, are fruit of my knowing.

Believing God delights in me, really believing, puts me in a completely different frame of mind. I've heard it said, "The more I delight in God, the more He delights in me." I'm learning to live this truth. Having God's approval is great for my future. Having His delight is great for my "now."

No doubt there are questions flashing through your mind about "what if's." What if someone isn't living as a child of God? What if someone does this or that differently? My question back to you would be, does it matter to God what another person does when He reflects on His relationship with you? This is the kind of thinking that occurs to our natural self and you will hear it from your children as they mature. In every case, point them back to God's delight in them, and emphasize the importance of obeying what He speaks into their life…because that will foster their delight in Him.

For those of you who are parents, perhaps you can easily identify with this idea? How many times have you told your children it doesn't matter what so-and-so family does, our family is not doing such and such. Or, "I don't care what Jenna's parents lets her do, you're not Jenna." You apply this naturally because as a parent, you understand the direction you want your child to go. Further, within your own family, you most likely have different ways to deal with your children. To them, on the surface it seems unfair, but in your wisdom, you deal with your children individually to bring out the best in them.

Though our Heavenly Father is flawless, all wise, and consistent, He tends to operate in a similar manner. He is able to delight in each of His children.

Every one of us can choose whether we want to live attached to God by a thread or by a thick cord. Or whether we have a superficial relationship with God or a deep one. Though getting a thicker cord or deeper relationship requires a measure of discipline, it requires a heap more of mutual delight.

Delight versus Discipline

So, why am I devoting an entire chapter to delight? Because we all need to be awakened to it, we need to experience it. Our children need to experience it too. We have spent years and years working on building consistency from the discipline angle and it has produced temporary results. I believe it's time to approach consistency from another angle.

I believe we need to foster a delight-first approach to prayer just as much if not more than a discipline-first approach. We are familiar with the discipline-first approach as evidenced by common statements like, "you have to/should pray every day." While that statement is true, there may be a better way to get that result. A delight-first approach encourages prayer in a way that suits a person's giftings, personality, and spiritual development. Believe me, if someone truly delights in prayer, a discipline in prayer will become evident.

We know from indications in the Gospels that Jesus would often separate Himself from His disciples to pray daily. These were times He spent communing with His Heavenly Father. He wasn't following Old Testament rules when He did this; He was following the delight of His heart. Was He disciplined? It looks that way. But I'm pretty sure it's safe to say He wasn't disciplined for discipline's sake. It's no surprise at key times in His life, His Heavenly Father poured out words of affirmation on Him, expressing His approval and delight.

Can we expect our Heavenly Father to send us words of affirmation today? Indeed, we can. There may not be a dove hovering over us, or clouds parting and words booming from the sky, but our Heavenly Father can most certainly express His delight in us through peace (Luke 2:14), in messages from His spirit to ours, through His Word, and even through daily events such as a spectacular sunset. If we know we can expect to hear Him, we will listen.

Just as I finished typing the last paragraph, my iPhone buzzed indicating I'd received a random out of the blue text from a dear friend. It said, "You are loved. Thought you should know." My Heavenly Father wished to illustrate this point Himself just now and I think he did a fabulous job.

If we are uninformed or misinformed about God's delight in us, we will most likely muddle our way through as Christians with self-effort, struggling with the most basic of spiritual development. We might live life motivated to escape hell, rather than motivated to move toward heaven. We might think our efforts are only about pleasing a frowning God, not enjoying a delightful One. We might mistakenly continue making all of life for God about us and not Him.

Informed And Educated

One summer I attended a prayer conference in Colorado Springs that literally changed my life. In one of the workshops I met the missions leader who runs the "Win 10/40" project (www.win1040.com). That session was revelatory on several levels for me, but Beverly Pegues taught me something about information and education in that workshop and during a few other encounters I feel I need to pass along.

Beverly shared, "the biggest problem with prayer mobilization is the lack of knowledge." People simply aren't informed enough to plug in to what God is doing around the world. The other key factor she explained, and I've proved it to be true, is that children are the easiest to educate for immediate action.

I've discovered that a preacher might preach something to a congregation for several weeks and perhaps get a little bump in action from the group. However, a children's minister can present some of the same material and get almost immediate results. I can't explain it, other than to say, children are hungry to do something and are ready to go when handed the opportunity. Over and over again I've seen this dynamic in play. It makes me truly grateful I've been called to work with children.

So, let's inform our children about God's delight in them and watch their reaction. Let's take the time to hammer it home and work it into as many lessons as possible, even if it means deviating from the same old stories we've told for years. Let's give them confidence to be sure of their salvation, communicating clearly and often with their God.

Let's not have another squirrelly generation when it comes to accepting God's delight. Let's choose to move beyond ourselves into a spiritual life that revolves around God and God alone.

God inhabits praise, dwells in the heavens, exists outside of time, and delights in me...always. When you believe this truth I hope you will be as inspired to share it with others, as I am inspired to share it with you.

QUESTIONS

1. Do you believe being filled with the Holy Spirit is all it takes for God to delight in you? If not, what steps must a person take to earn God's delight?

2. Is what you believe about God's delight in sync with what you teach?

3. Take a few moments to make a mental or written list of Old Testament Bible stories you've shared with children. Now eliminate any that do not reveal or display the attribute of God's delight. How many stories are left?

FURTHER READING

1. ***God Without Religion*** by Andrew Farley
   Written by a pastor who is learning that religion actually gets in the way of relationship with God. Andrew shares how to have a relationship that is based on God and not a religion surrounding Him.

2. ***Cat & Dog Theology*** by Bob Sjogren
   A "sticky" (easy to remember/apply) analogy of how Christians relate to God. Full of insight that will help with KP training, especially praying from God's perspective.

3. ***Captivating*** by John and Stasi Eldredge
   Primarily written to women who have struggled with self-image and performance-based approval. Full of valuable information that can be applied to help prevent negative patterns from being set in children.

Chapter 10: SPIRITUAL EARS

I was in China when the first iPhone was unveiled in 2008, so I missed much of the buzz around the new device. However, being an Apple fan, I kept my eye on it from afar, and tried to keep from drooling on my keyboard. It wasn't long until I started seeing posts on Facebook made from iPhones and received emails with little "Sent from my iPhone" tag lines at the bottom. Millions of phones have been sold to date, and I'm sure it's safe to say thousands of users still don't know all the functions, hidden tricks and features of the phone. I've seen a lot of links to "hidden iPhone tricks" and now that I finally own one, I've taken a peek at some of them.

Hidden features. We have a few of them ourselves.

As humans, we were designed with a pair of external ears near the brain that makes navigating the natural world easier on us. They allow us to listen to sounds and people around us and pass along vital information to the brain. Through extrapolation, it is known we humans are also equipped with a second kind of ear, an internal one, near the heart. This kind of ear allows us to listen to the sounds of heaven to hear from God. Though I am not sure what this ear, or ears, looks like, I know it/they function to receive signals directly from God's spirit to ours.

We are designed to hear from God. You and I not only "can" hear God's voice, but we were designed for it. However, as people born into a natural world, learning to use our spiritual ears takes practice. Just as a baby takes time to make sense of all the auditory signals it receives, it takes time for us to initialize our spiritual ears before we can begin enjoying the sounds of heaven.

Testing 1, 2, 3

At a Missions Fest several years ago, one of the speakers asked the question, "When was the last time you heard from God? Was it when your pastor preached?" Hands all over the large auditorium shot up. I seemed they were proud of themselves for having attended church somewhere within the past week. After a few heartbeats, the speaker responded, "Shame on you!" I breathed a sigh of relief. My hand wasn't up because I had a sneaking suspicion it was a trick question. But the truth is, it could have been.

I thought his next stop would have been something about us hearing from God by reading His Word; I stood a better chance at hitting that one. But he skipped right over that and went straight for the question that left me feeling like a two-dimensional cardboard Christian. "How many of you have heard God's voice in the past 24 hours?" Youch! Again, my hand stayed down; this time because I didn't deserve to raise it.

So what's changed since then? I *believe* God can speak to me. I've *accepted* He wants me to listen to Him. And as a result, I have *taken steps* to learn to hear His voice. Over time I've learned how to put myself in a position to hear, and through support from nurturing friends I have found ways to start walking in *alignment* with what I hear Him speak. I am listening more than ever with my spiritual ears.

Bypassing The Brain

One of the biggest obstacles any of us face when trying to hear God's voice is our own brain. It's what makes us question whether or not it was God who spoke, and nine times out of ten, dissuades us from taking action. There is a kind of spiritual override that needs to occur when God speaks, but until you learn where that lever is within you, it's difficult if not impossible, to clearly hear.

I'll never forget the day it dawned on me how significant it is that God, who is a spirit, chooses to speak to my spirit directly without audibly routing His signal through my ears. I was presenting this very content when it hit me that God prefers to communicate spirit to spirit, completely bypassing our brains by leaving out our ears. At the time I was holding one big ear near my stomach and another big ear up in the air, trying to get across what God had just dropped into my heart.

I am not saying God doesn't communicate with us through our ears, just that it seems He prefers spirit-to-spirit, mano-a-mano, communication. Nothing gets lost in translation this way. There's no, "Thus saith the Lord," to make you tremble; just a knowing that comes from the pit of your stomach.

Lost In Translation

How do we translate God's spiritual language into something our brains can process? I don't know if it's possible. It seems like every single time I recognize God speaking to me, if my brain gets ahold of it first I begin to "think" about it and my brain starts putting up roadblocks.

I guess this is why He prefers to speak into my spirit. I'm still trying to train myself to react from a spirit level, then process. If what I hear in my spirit doesn't sound like God or line up with the Word, I ignore it. When I recognize God's voice, if I process it through my brain then react, it's like I'm putting the cart before the horse. Sometimes I'll do the right thing, but mostly I get stuck, make the wrong move, or make the right move too late.

Having just returned from spending five years in China, I'm still sorting through language anomalies. You may even find a few in this book, or hear a few if you ever hear me speak. While there I had to learn to speak Putonghua (Mandarin) enough to get around and communicate for making friends, shopping, tutoring, and handling work and church related business. Let me tell you from personal experience, a lot can get lost in translation. And a lot can go unsaid.

There were times I wondered if God ever experienced a frustration similar to mine as I tried to get very foreign concepts across in a language that wasn't built to express them. How God must ache to be able to clearly communicate ideas foreign to our religious framework with language that can't quite grasp the intent of heaven. It's no wonder He wants us to worship Him in spirit and truth and it's no wonder we hear Him best with our spiritual ears.

Think about the hundreds of sermons you've heard and the level of response you've experienced. When your ears are engaged, so is your brain, reasoning, arguing, defending, and whirling away with every spoken word. However, think of the times when the Holy Spirit has nudged you into doing something…that was God speaking to you. Have there been times when you "went with your gut" about something? Chances are, that was God moving you in a language your spirit could respond to without overthinking, or engaging your brain.

Your Second Brain

It shouldn't come as a shock to you that I am a reader. When a friend of mine suggested a book for me, *Who Switched Off My Brain* by Dr. Caroline Leaf, I had no idea what a treasure trove it would become. In it, one of the most peculiar things I discovered was about my heart, not my brain. In Chapter 4, the author explains, our heart is more than a pump. It functions as a second brain with it's own independent nervous system. Additionally, it releases a balancing hormone that regulates many of our brain's functions and stimulates our behavior.

What a cool bit of science to go along with what the Holy Spirit was teaching me. For those of you reluctant to give up control to your heart, fearing your brain would be disengaged, think again. Your heart is a brain, a primitive one, but a brain nevertheless. Scientifically speaking, the heart controls how the other bigger brain functions and actually stimulates our behavior. We need to let it do its job more often.

These days being led by the Holy Spirit, being tethered spirit-to-spirit with the God of all creation doesn't stress me out. It seems He thought of everything. But it takes practice to learn to navigate the spiritual world from the confines of our natural one. Some say practice makes perfect, but in this regard, I've experienced how practice makes…comfortable.

Practice Makes Comfortable

I've been told that my being a woman gives me a slight advantage in the area of listening to God because I no doubt was born equipped with a dose of "woman's intuition." Which by the way, I am learning to pay more attention to these days. It's not spooky, or new age, but it is something I'm learning not to ignore. If this is a tool God gave me as a woman, then I need to embrace it and use it to its fullest potential, whatever that might be.

Whether male or female, the thing about learning to hear God's voice is we need to practice doing just that. The more we practice hearing His voice, the more comfortable we will feel in obeying.

When we are able to trust what we hear, sure of where it comes from, we can act with assurance.

I recently read somewhere of a good Christian man who nearly went berserk the night before his wedding. He *knew* the woman he was marrying was right for him, but he was waiting for God to give His okay with a special sign. He didn't get a special sign, but went ahead with the wedding. As it turns out, it was the right move. His *knowing* could have been enough, but he was waiting for an external sign.

Why do we go looking for signs and confirmations when we have a "knowing" given to us in our spirit? Because of fear and lack of familiarity mostly, and at times, perhaps because we want to be double-dog-sure before we act. There's a reason for that last one. Sometimes, obedience to what we hear is, well, a little crazy.

Crazy Obedience

Francis Chan has written a beautiful book entitled *Crazy Love*. As much as I enjoyed his book, and would suggest it to anyone looking to bust out of religious complacency, I wanted to drop a few paragraphs on you about something else, crazy obedience.

Here is where stories from the Old Testament can come to the rescue. Think of all the crazy things the OT heroes did, like build an ark, make iron float, create a drought, marry an unfaithful wife on purpose, hold out a staff to part a sea, and visit a king without invitation. Just ask Gideon; sometimes God gets the biggest kick out of crazy. Crazy obedience.

To me, crazy obedience is obedience that just doesn't add up or make sense in the natural way of seeing things.

In the New Testament crazy obedience crops up again in the life of Jesus and the NT church. Jesus accepted the cross, Paul took a boat he knew would be wrecked, John penned what the Angel showed him, and Peter went to Cornelius. There's more, but you get the idea.

What about in present day America, Africa, Asia, Central and South America, Europe or the Middle East? Absolutely, in all of these places God is still speaking and people are listening and obeying with crazy obedience.

While in Bali, Indonesia for a 10/40 Window conference, I heard and saw one of the most heart wrenching stories of crazy obedience. An Indonesian Christian publically professed her forgiveness toward Muslims who had nearly devastated her life. This woman had crawled out of a burning church, escaping only to be shot at point blank range in the face by a Muslim who helped set the fire. Her act of forgiveness was an act of obedience, crazy obedience, to Christ.

In my home church, Zack Tracy and I engaged in some joint crazy obedience before I left for China. Zack wrote what he felt God told him on a get-well card for Larry, who was struck down suddenly with liver disease. What he wrote scared me, but I delivered the card. That was crazy obedience. Curious about what Zack wrote? He simply scrawled, "You will be home in three days." No way was that humanly possible. But three days after I delivered the card Larry was home because with God nothing is impossible.

Larry is fine today, because of a God who would get more glory from him being alive than being with Him...and perhaps because of our crazy obedience too. Larry says Zack's card got him through very difficult hours.

Crazy obedience comes in all shapes and sizes. It puts a ring in the offering, it holds its tongue, it speaks up, it walks instead of rides, it shops, it whispers prayers, it writes texts, it buys cars, it sings new songs, it preaches, it hugs, it throws shoes in the ocean; it even hangs on a cross. As you are faithful to obey in the small things, hang on, because He will trust you with His big, big heart. And that will require crazy obedience.

Crazy obedience has never been in more demand than now. And in the days ahead it will be an increasingly precious commodity of the Church.

End Time Necessity

As I mentioned in Chapter 1, as I near the finish line of the end time, I need to be sure I make my relationship with God about bringing Him glory rather than getting what I want. This means I need to hear from God clearly to live in alignment. I also need to be sure my relationships with others are more about bringing glory to God than meeting my own needs. Why? Because of what's headed our way. You can feel it too, can't you?

If we had the chance to sit down together, I with a cold Coke Zero and a bag of Puffed Cheetos, and you with your favorite drink and snack, in addition to kids prayer stuff, I'd love to talk a little eschatology with you. Seriously. I'm fascinated with the study of the end times (eschatology), especially since I'm convinced I'm living in them.

I'm not a scholar, but the reality of where our world is headed and the timing of events unfolding make it hard for me to look the other way. If ever there was a time for a strong prayer force, that time is now and eschatology plays a bigger role than most people realize. If nothing else, it connects us to an urgency coursing through the global Body of Christ.

I am pretty well convinced the rapture isn't quite the escape hatch people have thought it would be. If I am right, being able to hear God's voice and being able to submit to crazy obedience will be two of the most desirable assets during the days leading up to Christ's second coming.

I am aware many people don't like to think about this, and others dismiss it out of hand. Some are scared to death of it like I was in primary school, while even others make certain positions linked to salvation. None of that matters to me much. All I know is I don't want to miss the Messiah's second coming the way the Jews missed His first one. Whatever is in store for the Church, I want to know it and walk in alignment with it. And I want to prepare my children to walk in alignment, hearing clearly what God has to say.

I want to get in as much listening practice as I can while things are easy so I can be sure and confident in days when we are in the thick of struggle. It's why I take time to listen before any major decision and why I've gotten into the habit of listening before any minor decision. I want to stay in good spiritual shape because the race set before me is leading right to the finish line of this era.

I want to finish the race well because I know my reward is Christ Himself. I want to experience His delight and bring Him more glory than humanly possible. Join me?

REAL LIFE STORIES

I know the idea of leading a "listening time" can be intimidating, especially if you've never seen one before. Following are four real life stories to help you get an idea of the reach of listening activities and how they can be used.

1. A Pink Cupcake

When I first tried a listening time of my own in a group, it was at a children's ministers training seminar several years ago. The adults in the room got quiet for a minute or so as we listened to get an impression, picture, word, or movie playing in our mind's eye. We did just what we would train children to do in the future.

As the leader solicited responses from attendees, I kept silent. I was curious to hear what others had to say, and a little embarrassed about what I "heard." People around me saw warrior angels and beams of light and all sorts of strange things. It seemed very spiritual to me at the time, especially because what I saw was nothing related. I saw a pink cupcake. And to make matters worse, I didn't have a clue what it meant.

I've shared this story with others during different training events in the past to help them understand "different is okay." However, about a year ago, nearly ten years after the first "sighting", I saw the pink cupcake again. This time it was with my eyes wide open as I watched children being filled with the Holy Spirit during a meeting in a closed Asian nation. With that moment came understanding.

So, what was that pink cupcake about? It was a promise God kept. I like sweets. I like cupcakes…a lot. God in His unique way was letting me know He was preparing a treat for me and was putting it right under my nose. The cupcake was so close to my eyes it was all I could see. A glorious pink cupcake. What better time to see it than when children in a closed nation were being filled by the Holy Spirit. Sweet! It was also a reminder to me of God's glory and delight.

Incidentally, within my first year of arriving in China, I went to a huge open market to do some card shopping. There's no Hallmark where I lived, so I was on a hunt. I found two purchase-worthy cards that day. One was a flower I could use as a gift. The other was, you guessed it, a large pink cupcake. I didn't want to forget. I still have that cupcake card. At the time it reminded me of a promise and gave me hope that some day, when the time was right, I'd understand. Today, I keep it as a testimony.

2. Double Portion

Jared attended Monday night kids prayer sessions at my local church during his primary school years. We changed our format to include listening time every single week. Jared, like everyone who attended, had his own special folder to put his drawings in after each listening time. This was our way of charting progress and finding themes in what children drew.

This particular night Jared drew a picture of a rainbow with someone praying over him. He said God showed him to ask for a double portion from someone named Jason. Jason Sciscoe. Jared didn't really know who Jason was, but might have heard his name in conversations. So, we explained Jason was an evangelist at the time. Jared was rather surprised, but very interested in this development.

Instead of putting the paper in his folder, he took it home that night and put it on his dresser. That's where it stayed for quite some time.

A while later, Jason Sciscoe came to Jared's home church for a weekend revival. It was then that Jared decided to be baptized, and he wanted Jason to do it. After the baptism, a beaming Jared shook Jason's hand as someone shared the story about the "double portion" with Jason.

With Jared's permission, Jason put his hands on Jared and prayed for him to receive a double portion of what God had given him. The air was electrified. And, as they prayed, someone snapped this photo.

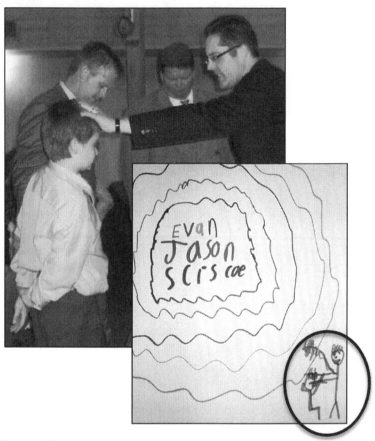

3. Ripped Paper

While in China my first year, I did some kp training among expats on Sundays in the home of friends. On the "ripped paper" Sunday a few people left a little freaked out, but in a good way.

I was running a few minutes late, so didn't have time to prepare half sheets of paper like I normally would have with scissors. So I folded the sheets I needed and ripped them in half by hand. There were a few jagged edges, but I figured it wouldn't matter. Well, I was in for a surprise, because in fact, it would matter.

During a family listening time (that day children and parents listened together) each person drew or wrote what God spoke to them on one of those ripped half sheets. As we shared what God spoke, excitement picked up as a mom shared her picture.

As it turned out, two people, a mom and a teenager from another family sitting in different parts of the room, drew almost identical pictures. They both understood what they had drawn and as they shared their pictures there were enough chill bumps to go around...and around.

As we closed the sharing and ministry time that day, the mom and teenager put their papers on the coffee table as I wanted to take photos of them for future reference. As they laid their papers down, I noticed something odd. The two ripped pieces of paper came together perfectly.

I doubled checked to be sure I wasn't imaging it then called everyone over to see it for themselves. As if drawing the same thing wasn't enough, God worked it so that what they drew was on the same original piece of paper.

The teenager left convinced; that ripped paper put him over the edge. As for the mom, she was letting tears flow down her cheeks, as she thanked God for His attention to detail.

"Pastor Leaman"

Now for the last story. It's a goodie. As I was leading a listening demonstration time with children from Singapore's Tabernacle of Joy, this story unfolded.

I had given the usual instructions. "Get quiet, then when I say, "Go!", draw or write the first thing you see. If you don't see anything, write the first color you see when you close your eyes." The children were in their places ready to go. Some were under tables, others were snuggled up to the perimeter walls, but they were spread out like I'd asked them to be. I was trying to eliminate any copy cats, a typical occurrence.

Within the first few seconds, children started drawing. Since this was a demonstration activity, the first time these children ever tried to listen for God's voice, I was looking for patterns. The first hurdle, obedience, was navigated. Now I was observing, preparing myself to follow any prompts by the Holy Spirit.

I noticed in one area of the room there was one different image on each page of three different boys. The boys were not near each other, just in the same part of the room. A fourth boy's paper caught my eye and was the "all is well" signal from the Holy Spirit. This boy's paper contained images from all three of the other boys' papers.

About this time, we concluded the activity, then had a sharing time. Nobody would willingly share, so I started them off by sharing what I'd noticed about Seth's paper having a combination of drawings from other children. Then the sharing started like a flood. Their faith was primed and children all around the room wanted share what they "got."

As they shared, I noticed a second pattern. Children in another part of the room drew parts of a similar scene. I don't remember all the details, but the collective idea was they had all drawn something related to a particular preacher "over the seas", but we didn't know who it was. After discussing our options, we decided to listen again to see what to pray for this preacher and if God wanted us to know who it was.

About 20 seconds into the next listening session, Seth came to me quietly, concerned about something. He was hearing a name over and over and wondered if it was his imagination or if it could be a message from God. I asked him the name and he said, "Well, I don't know if it's real."

I assured him it wasn't a problem, so he told me the name. "Pastor Leaman." I assured him it was a real name and he seemed quite elated that a name he'd never heard before must have come from God. After the listening time, we all huddled around Seth and decided we should pray for Pastor Leaman and though we didn't know exactly how to pray, we tried to hit the highlights; health and protection.

Needless to say, the kids and I were psyched! After our session was over, I shared what happened with a friend, Cylinda Nickel who was there doing some work with missionary kids. Immediately, Cylinda knew why Seth heard this name. Pastor Leaman was having serious health problems and was in need of prayer.

The next morning, Cylinda stopped by to share this information with the group. You should have seen them glow. They were so excited that they offered to pray for Cylinda and even did a listening time for her right on the spot. The three children who "got" something for her shared and all of it made sense to her, even though it seemed disjointed to us.

As a result, a ripple effect started. Cylinda took the news back to "Pastor Leaman," and I took the story back to Seth's Sunday school teachers. And that was the beginning of something wonderful.

As a result, the concept of listening for God's voice is no longer a foreign concept to children at Tabernacle of Joy and the prayers of children half way around the world touched Pastor Leaman and his family.

QUESTIONS

1. How does God usually speak to you? How regularly do you hear His voice?

2. In what respect is obedience connected to hearing God's voice?

3. What might crazy obedience in your life look like?

FURTHER READING

1. ***You Can Hear God's Voice, Really*** by John Eldridge
   Full of practical stories and experience you can glean from.

2. ***Hearing God Curriculum*** by Becky Fischer
   (www.kidsinministry.com)
   Contained in this curriculum are 13 weeks worth of object lessons and practical applications. Previously titled, "School of the Holy Spirit," it's one of the best curriculums I know of to help initialize the spiritual ears in children.

3. ***www.endtime.com*** by Irvin Baxter
   This website carries digital downloads of comprehensive, easy to understand videos which show how the book of Revelation is unfolding right under our noses. One of my favorites is the one explaining the Seven Trumpets.

Chapter 11: NEW CREATURES

I know this paragraph will generate eye rolls, but I'm going to write it anyway. I enjoy Sci-Fi, and if you don't, I feel a bit sorry for you. In the words of the imaginary Anne Shirley, the world of Sci-Fi has "so much scope for imagination." There goes the eye roll. Who would have thought Anne Shirley could be linked somehow to Sci-Fi? And why on earth am I starting a chapter on the Holy Spirit with science fiction? Bear with me at least a paragraph longer.

I don't think calling myself a fan would be accurate, but I sure do enjoy me some Star Trek, Star Wars, and anything a little "ET phone home." The Word says we become new creatures and I guess I'm one who takes that literally. In fact, I was kind of bummed when I discovered Paul said I would look like myself in my glorified body. I was hoping for something a little sleeker, not so hippy, if you know what I mean.

Seriously, the fact is, when we are filled with the Holy Spirit, we begin to truly live life as the spiritual beings we are. Though wrapped in flesh, the real me was infused with something heavenly that has the capacity to alter my DNA. My natural DNA.

Yes, you read that right. My spirit infused with the Holy Spirit has the capacity to alter my natural DNA. Wow! Sound like something from another galaxy to you? How about something from the One who flung all the galaxies out there in the first place.

Spiritual DNA

Over the past several years I've heard a few speakers refer to something called, "Spiritual DNA." From what I can gather, some are referring to the beliefs that make a person unique in the Body of Christ, while others are referring to the infilling of the Holy Spirit as new spiritual DNA. In John 3:6, John writes, *"Humans can reproduce only human life, but the Holy Spirit gives birth to spiritual life."*

This is a fascinating thing to consider. The very building blocks that made Jesus who He is, are some of the same building blocks we acquire when we are filled with the Holy Spirit.

> *"But to all who believed him and accepted him, he gave the right to become children of God. They are reborn—not with a physical birth resulting from human passion or plan, but a birth that comes from God"* (John 1:12-13).

While this idea of new DNA from heaven is fascinating, I find the altering of my human DNA by the power of the Holy Spirit is mind blowing. In her book, *Who Switched Off My Brain*, Dr. Caroline Leaf, reveals scientific evidence confirming Romans 12:2 to be accurate. Our human DNA can be changed by our thoughts in a process called "retranscribing neuroplastically." As our thoughts change, our genetic code begins to morph into something new, even something we can pass down to the next generation. Through the power of the Holy Spirit, not only is my spirit turbo charged, but my natural self begins an evolution of sorts.

As I stay full of the Holy Spirit, I evolve through the power of the Holy Spirit into the real version of myself God envisioned before I was born. This is not something that happens as a result of my best self-help efforts, but is a natural evolution that occurs when I relinquish control of my mortal self to God. The work of the Holy Spirit is to comfort and guide me during this process.

Altered Human DNA

How is my natural DNA being altered? By thoughts, mostly, and by modified behavior. The study of epigenetics, a relatively new area of scientific study, demonstrates how things outside the double helix of a DNA strand can alter its effects, or genes. It is quite commonly accepted knowledge today that our emotions generated by our thoughts impact us down to our cellular level. Our thoughts have the power to turn genes off and on, impacting our DNA. Talk about becoming a new creature!

We need to understand being full of the Holy Spirit means we are no longer victims of our biology or heredity. Our thoughts and beliefs, attitudes and actions impact whether or not we are evolving spiritually toward Christ or at a stand still. We are what we think; it seems even Solomon knew this.

"For as he thinks in his heart, so is he" (Proverbs 23:7, NLV).

It's safe to say the Apostle Paul didn't have this 21st century scientific research to back him up when he wrote the Philippian church about watching their thought life. If my thoughts influence me down to my cellular level, and if they affect my mental and physical health, then I too, need Paul's advice.

"And now, dear brothers and sisters, one final thing. Fix your thoughts on what is true, and honorable, and right, and pure, and lovely, and admirable. Think about things that are excellent and worthy of praise" (Philippians 4:8).

You and I have the capacity to the let the Holy Spirit work in our lives to such a degree that our very DNA can be altered. More importantly, that same altered DNA can be passed on to future generations. This is most likely why the God of Creation told His people over and over how their actions would impact subsequent generations. It wasn't just the *result* of their actions that would affect future generations, but it was their very thoughts, attitudes, and behavior that had impact. In a sense, one generation has the capacity to hotwire the genetic code of future generations in a positive or negative way.

There are a few things to take away from all this scientific mumbo-jumbo. First, as new creatures in Christ, we are no longer victims of our biology or heredity. We can no longer get away with making excuses for our thoughts and resulting mental and physical health. When you see children being snagged in this ancient mind trap, remind them of who they are in Christ and how, through the Holy Spirit, they have power to choose to be victorious.

Secondly, each generation has the capacity to directly impact the next at a cellular level. To me, that's huge. I don't have children of my own, but I can imagine I would have loved to have known this when my children were still running around in diapers. It isn't limited to progeny, your direct descendants. Your thought-induced behavior influences the children you train as well.

Fruit of the Spirit

As your DNA evolves, proof of what's going on inside is manifest on the outside by way of spiritual fruit. Staying full of the Holy Spirit is, "good for health." Everyone knows fruit is healthy.

As you have no doubt figured out by now, I have spent some time living and working in China. One of the most common phrases I heard during my first year was, "Angie, that's bad for health." This is because I drank cold drinks, even in winter, and would have a small bag of chips for a snack. They preferred I sip a scalding hot beverage, even in summer, and slurp up mandarin orange sections for a snack.

In order to help us recognize proof of our spiritual evolution, the Holy Spirit inspired Paul to write about the fruit of the Spirit. Have you ever taken a look at that list and thought, "Oh wow! I don't stand a chance." I have. I want to evolve into that. I've already learned it's impossible for me to self-help, or zip-tie that fruit into my life.

> *"But the Holy Spirit produces this kind of fruit in our lives: love, joy, peace, patience, kindness, goodness, faithfulness, gentleness, and self-control. There is no law against these things"* (Galatians 5:22-23).

Do you see who produces the fruit? My name is not in that verse, and neither is yours. It's the handiwork of the Holy Spirit. Do you see what kind of fruit it produces? It produces fruit that is literally good for your health.

Take a look at that list from Galatians again, and think about the opposite fruit. Maybe you have noticed there is a direct link between several diseases and the opposite attributes on the list? Bad fruit, such as hatred, sadness, anxiety, cruelty, wickedness, flakiness, harshness, and blame (unforgiveness), are linked by many in the medical profession to *stress* which is the perpetrator of many familiar diseases.

For the heart, stress can cause high blood pressure, hardening of the arteries, aneurysms and strokes. Immune systems are compromised by stress from unforgiveness, resentment, and bitterness; this stress can cause a person's body to turn on itself. Even our digestive systems can be struck by the stresses of a daily life not producing spiritual fruit. IBS, and every other stomach and intestinal discomfort could very well be an indicator that something is out of whack in your thought life.

The good news is, the more you pay attention to your thoughts and use the advice of Philippians 4:8, the more balanced your emotions will be, making it possible for the fruit of the Spirit to flourish in your life.

By allowing the Holy Spirit to produce good fruit in you, not only are you impacting a future generation, you are quite possibly lengthening your life so you'll be around to see it. The fruit of the Spirit is truly good for health.

New Tongues

I've often wondered why God chose the most heathen muscle in my body to be the one thing He wants to control. I guess He likes a challenge. My tongue has gotten me into more trouble in my lifetime than I care to admit. And it's the part of me God wants as proof to unbelievers that He is real and in charge.

> *"So you see that speaking in tongues is a sign, not for believers, but for unbelievers"* (1 Corinthians 14:22a).

When I was a child, I used to think if I could speak in tongues it would be proof I was going to heaven. As it turns out, I didn't have much in the way of proof because I couldn't get the hang of yielding myself to God. Because of this, I lived life trying to please God every other way I could think of. I was scared to die and I was scared of the rapture. It was a near disaster. Only God's grace and the prayers of my parents kept me.

You see, I was a very independent child, and tried to do all the Spirit's work myself. Perhaps you have met a child like this? I had an idea in my head that I needed to be something like all the heroes of the Bible thrown together in one person. It was exhausting and I failed miserably every single day. I tried to be good enough on my own, but because I hadn't learned to yield myself to God, I was truly on my own.

Over time I learned to yield myself and my tongue to God. What helped me the most was being around others who knew how to do this without being too weird about it. It was slow going, but one evening, I got help from a friend with a simple demonstration.

A dear friend of mine took the time to show me how unyielding I was after she came to pray with me during an altar call. I was standing at the front, hands up, eyes and mouth closed. After a few minutes of prayer that went nowhere, she got my attention and showed me her fist. "Angie, you are as closed as my fist." My exterior posture of hands up and eyes closed, masked my unresponsive, hard and closed spirit. In an instant I saw what she meant and it helped me tremendously to adjust.

I've learned my speaking in tongues is not a proof of my salvation nor a spiritual ticket to heaven. It is a sign for unbelievers, a better way to worship and intercede and it builds up my inner self. I have discovered the more I release myself to God in this way, the easier it becomes.

You might be wondering if I speak in tongues every day. The answer is yes, especially when I'm driving alone or if I'm feeling overwhelmed. While living in China, I prayed in tongues under my breath often, especially in moments of frustration or fear. It's not usually an eyes closed tight, fist shaking, tears streaming kind of experience. Just something I can flip into as I'm going about my day. And I don't make a big deal of it, just something I do "under the radar." I didn't know it was possible until I heard Stacey Campbell talk about doing something similar during a kids seminar a few years back. At the time I thought, "Hmm. That would be cool." Yeah, it is.

You will no doubt run into people who have been taught yielding to God to the extent the Holy Spirit can pray through them isn't possible. Or perhaps they have been taught speaking in tongues is one of the gifts of the Spirit and not meant for everyone. What you need to know is unless they become hungry for more or God causes them to yield to this extent, they will go with what they know. However, it's not quite what Paul taught.

> *"So, my dear brothers and sisters, be eager to prophesy, and don't forbid speaking in tongues"* (1 Corinthians 14:39).

Too Much Of A Good Thing

What Paul taught was that speaking in tongues was good and he did it a lot, but prophesying was better in a group setting. On a few occasions, he wrote to address the problem of people running around praying in tongues all the time. They were making absolutely no sense to anyone so he informed them about the use of tongues in a corporate setting.

I ran into a similar situation with a kids group once, so I get Paul's point. They went to pray for someone's healing, but they were all jibber jabbering in tongues, giving absolutely no intelligible encouragement to the person they were praying for. I was clueless about what was being said and so was the person being prayed for.

So, I stopped the praying mid-stride. I explained that for personal edification, praying in tongues from start to finish is perfectly fine. But when praying for healing, to edify, to encourage someone, most often it will need to be done in that person's first language if possible. We started the prayer back up, they adjusted with some difficulty, but when they used that person's first language, the person responded.

The point is, speak in tongues as often as you like in any situation or during any activity. A great time to practice, yes practice, is when vacuuming so you won't be distracted by what you sound like. Though you won't know what you're saying, your spirit might. When in a group setting, if ministry is involved, such as praying for the sick, praying to edify, lending some encouragement or giving a blessing, use that person's first language.

Though the Holy Spirit can move on you, or influence you to pray in a particular way or intensity, remember you are still in control of your body. So, be aware of surroundings and don't try to make every speaking in tongues encounter a "Thus Saith the Lord" moment.

Prophesying

Speaking of Prophesy, something interesting happened in a kids' prayer meeting down in Texas. First a little background. In some churches, they allow the practice of prophesying during a service. This entails someone giving a message in tongues and that person or another giving an interpretation. This usually serves to get a message across to the congregation at a higher intensity than what was spoken behind the pulpit. It is also tends to happen as a hushed or sacred moment in more traditional churches.

In that particular kids' prayer meeting, three children and two teachers took time to listen at some point in their time together. When they came back together to share what they heard they were surprised everyone heard the same thing. Instead of giving a message in tongues with an interpretation to give a message, God simply gave the same message to each person there taking time to listen.

I wonder if that same dynamic could be at work in congregations around the world today? Some have bemoaned the lack of "tongues and interpretation" in churches these days, but I have to wonder if more of the congregation is listening for Him. Perhaps He is getting more delight by speaking the same thing to individuals.

Ultimately our lives are best-lived bringing glory to God. The very best way to do that is to be full of the Holy Spirit. To be full, is to be yielded. Speaking in tongues is indeed a miraculous gift and according to Peter, it's for you, and your children (Acts 2:39).

There is so much more to the work of the Holy Spirit. I've just tried to touch on the areas that might encourage you to step a little further into the water than you've ever gone before. We are indeed new creatures through Christ!

REAL LIFE STORIES

Following are three real life stories to help you process a few angles on this idea of being a new creature. Using our spiritual ears, yielding to God, and providing a sign for unbelievers.

1. Alignment

I'd heard a story or two about what it might mean to walk in "alignment" but I wasn't sure how to apply the information to myself. So, one fine day I drove a friend to a drive-in restaurant for an awesome Dr. Pepper and a chat. We were on the way to her brother's house for dinner, but were a bit early, so made the brief stop.

As we were talking about this very topic of alignment, my hand reached to start up the car. Simultaneously, my friend's phone rang. By the time I knew what was going on with the call, we were just rolling over the exit to the drive-in. My friend smiled and told me, "That was my brother. I told him we are already on the way."

I had no idea it was time to go. I was reacting before processing and from that experience, I started to know what it feels like to be in alignment. It's a moment I refer to often if I'm unsure. It's inspired a personal goal for me to walk in alignment *more* than humanly possible.

2. Jumping Off A Cliff

We had just finished an intense time of intercession during kids prayer. It was the night we prayed for child soldiers and children saw guns jamming and feet running away from doors. It was amazing. Natalie had prayed hard and with much intensity, but she hadn't ever prayed in tongues before, so didn't know how to yield to the Holy Spirit.

As children were filing out to meet their parents, Natalie expressed how she wished she could pray in tongues too, because there was so much she felt to pray, but didn't know how to say it. Cynthia heard her and offered on the spot to show her what to do. She said, "I can show you what to do in less than two minutes, if you want." My curiosity was piqued.

Cynthia definitely could move in and out of tongues without a problem, so I was listening intently too. Cynthia told Natalie, "It's kind of like running hard, then jumping off a cliff. You have to just let yourself go." So, she instructed Natalie to pray compliments to God, and when she ran out of words to say, to keep her mouth open, so she'd be ready to speak in tongues.

We stopped Natalie a few times because she kept going into intercession for missionaries, etc., but after she started giving compliments to God like Cynthia suggested, she stopped and said, "I'm letting gooooooooo." And off she went, over the cliff so to speak, rattling off praise in tongues. She stopped and said, "Wow! Can I do that again?" "Of course you can. Just jump off that cliff again," said Cynthia.

Well, it worked. And I've used it many times since, so feel free to try it for yourself.

QUESTIONS

1. How is the Holy Spirit good for your health?

2. Are you presenting the proverbial fruit of the Spirit? If so, in which areas? If not, what is preventing you?

3. What is your Holy Spirit to self-effort ratio? And how does one affect the other?

4. How comfortable are you with speaking in tongues? If you are comfortable, are you willing to lead children in this area? If you aren't comfortable, what do you plan to do about it?

FURTHER READING

1. **Who Switched Off My Brain** by Dr. Caroline Leaf
   This one is great for general information about how our brain works and is a huge help in understanding how we can truly and scientifically become new creatures through Christ.

2. **Holy Bible**
   1 Corinthians 14, and the book of Acts 2, 10, and 19.

Chapter 12: TOWARD DE LIGHT

Like moths to a flame, children were drawn to Jesus. It's peculiar to me how Jesus, a single man, nurtured this by giving instructions to His close friends to let children come near. How many guys do you know would encourage children to barge in on them? Many things about Jesus in the Gospels make me smile, but this one touches my heart.

Matthew 21 starts out with a bang as Jesus gave His disciples a prophetic word coupled with instructions. By verse six, His prophetic word was complete. By verse eight, adoring fans were throwing down their cloaks and cutting down palm branches to pave the wave for Him as He entered Jerusalem on a colt. Jesus appears to have made a beeline for the temple to give it the clean sweep it had desperately needed for a long time. Miracles followed as space made from the overturned tables allowed the blind and crippled access to Jesus.

Children in the vicinity responded to the electricity in the air as only children can. They didn't swallow it down, or rub away the goose bumps. They were running all over the place in the excitement of it all, screaming and hollering, most likely even in places reserved for reverent whispers. "Praise God for the Son of David!" rang out all through the temple grounds. They were drawn to the Light of the World (John 8:12, 9:5). And the religious leaders didn't like it. Not one bit.

When the religious men had enough of all the screaming and giggling and running around, their annoyance turned to indignation aimed at Jesus. They finally asked Him, *"Do you hear what these children are saying?"* (Matthew 21: 16). I love Jesus' reply. To these ultra religious, extremely proper men, Jesus challenged their knowledge of Scripture, then quoted from Psalm 8:2, *"You have taught children and infants to give you praise."* Bazinga! Can you hear the sizzle?

In one fell swoop, the Light of the World opened His mouth and unloaded with laser accuracy, dispelling darkness. Darkness that says, "Children should be seen and not heard." Darkness that even today insists on slandering the heritage of Jesus. In a sense, we see here how children picked up Jesus' energy on their spiritual radar, and broadcast it, amplified it, with their mouths. In this case, shouting out the truth in the face of religiosity.

Were God's enemies silenced? It seems Jesus' response was the last word on the matter, as no further retorts from the religious leaders were recorded.

It won't be any different today. Children are still children, and in my experience, no matter what continent they live on, or what their background, they have keen spiritual radar, antennas perpetually up. Getting them in the proximity of Jesus is our job. Once there, He will do the rest. Expect there to be running, giggling and shouting involved.

What About Grown-Ups?

I want to be like that. Drawn to my life's source of light and energy on an instinctual level, a spiritual level. But I find my schedule and my perceptions of God get in the way. How do I retune my spiritual radar, not only to detect Jesus, but also to transmit through my physical body and emotions the surge that comes with locking onto His spirit? I move toward delight, navigating my life by way of Jesus, the One in whom there is no darkness (1 John 1:5).

Transverse Orientation

I am a semi-nocturnal human, which means I enjoy staying up late at night. But that doesn't make me a nocturnal creature. For example, a moth. As such I have no internal navigation systems to pilot my life via the stars…or porch lights. And that is a good thing. It would be disconcerting to see me crash landing into your porch light would it not? Please don't get an image.

As someone often in search of a good memory hook, I've discovered moths might hold the key for this one. They may not be good for sweaters or wool, but since I'm writing and not knitting, let's take a deeper look. This will lead us slightly astray from the opening sentence, temporarily drawing us deeper into the navigational habits of moths. Yippee!

Moths, being nocturnal creatures, are thought to use a navigation system called transverse orientation that has an interesting application here. Transverse orientation is the act of keeping a fixed angle on a distant source of light. Additionally, this type of navigation is done individually, meaning moths don't fly like geese in formation.

For example, if a moth fixes on the moon and heads west, as long as it keeps the moon to its right, it will arrive at a westward destination because the moon moves across the horizon of the night sky. However, if it fixes on a false navigational light, say a porch light, it will go in circles because the light doesn't move across the sky, but is stationary. This leads to the eventual crash and burn so many of us are familiar with in summer months.

This little moth analogy serves to remind me of two important things. As I move toward delight I need to make sure I fix my angle of flight on the true navigational Light for my life and not something else that will ultimately lead to my demise. I move toward delight as I fix my eyes on Christ. Just ask Peter, the one who walked on water as long as he kept His eyes on Jesus. Secondly, this is something I have to do as an individual. I can't rely on others to get me where I want to go, flying blindly. In some ways this journey is a group endeavor, but at the end of the day, I am responsible to arrive at my destination. If I don't, it's on me.

My destination is interestingly enough the same as yours. It's the point wherein our lives reflect the most glory of God. It is a point where our hopes, dreams, consciousness, words, thoughts, actions, reactions and our very DNA are completely saturated by God's glory. And, in that moment, we will be changed to be like Him.

> *"...And let us run with endurance the race God has set before us. We do this by keeping our eyes on Jesus, the champion who initiates and perfects our faith..."* (Hebrews 12:1-2).

Moving Toward Delight

If you want that giggling and shouting childlikeness when in the presence of Jesus, discovering the "awe" in our awesome God is the surest route. Set your course there, navigating by the Light of your life. Visit the first few chapters of Genesis for an opening taste of delight, and then move on to Google for more. If Genesis and Google aren't working for you, pick up an old prayer journal or take a walk down memory lane. Remembering how far you've come will get you there too. If you're not thrilled, it's because you're most likely stuck in "Me Ville."

Moving toward "De Light" means getting out of "Me Ville."

As I'm sure you would agree, worship is making things about God, the One who rightfully deserves all the attention. Everything we do is to bring glory to God. Everything He asks us to do is ultimately to bring Him glory. That He can orchestrate such massive goodness on a large scale is simply amazing!

I just Goggled "Amazing Creation Facts," and discovered quite a few interesting things. Some of this stuff belongs in "Ripley's Believe It Or Not!"

When it comes to even numbers, watermelons have an even number of stripes on the rind; oranges an even number of segments; corn, an even number of rows per cob; wheat, an even number of grains per stalk. Even ocean waves roll to shore an even number of times (26) every minute in any weather.[1]

And there's this choice quote about the human brain. "Your brain has 100 thousand billion electrical connections, in other words, more electrical connections than all the electrical appliances on the face of the earth, yet it fits in a quart jar and operates for 70 years on 10 watts of power fueled by cheeseburgers and French fries!"[2]

See what I mean? Maybe facts like this seem like unusable trivia? Perhaps they are, but when we reflect on them, it is possible to receive a sense of awe about the undeniable "amazingness" of God. That sense of amazing is where living a life of worship springs from. It moves me towards delight and away from myself.

So maybe trivia isn't your thing. How about something a little more personal? Stories from the past, whether it is minutes or decades old, can serve to remind you of how God has stood by you and come to your rescue. These stories, written or remembered are powerful forces that can build awe and move you away from self-dependence, back into the Light of Jesus.

If trivia and reflecting on things God has done in the past don't jump start a little churning in your spirit, then perhaps it's because you're navigating through cloudy skies and are having difficulty seeing the Light. Don't feel left out, or give yourself an excuse not to worship. There's a remedy for this, speaking Light into your situation.

Let There Be Light!

Five months before I left China, the Holy Spirit began nudging me, letting me know it was time to go. I was having trouble seeing clearly the path ahead, and was getting a little concerned. I'd acted on the prompting by giving my notice, but unlike the moths I wrote about earlier, was having trouble locking onto the source of Light for my flight westward. My transverse orientation was taking a while to engage. John Luc Picard would have been frustrated!

It was during this time I heard from a friend. She encouraged me to speak, "Let There Be Light!" into my situation. The idea came from a book she'd read and applied by Cindy Trimm, *Commanding Your Morning.* (Though I am responsible for reaching my destiny, it sure is nice to have friends traveling ahead who can radio back good intel.)

So, I started praying and saying, "Let There Be Light!" about every little thing. I wanted to train myself to have a go-to response for life's cloudy days. I prayed light into the cloudy details of my future, and then in time into the haze. I continued doing so with patience rejoicing a lot when clarity came. I prayed light into relationships, so I would know how to proceed, and it seems the right light came at the right time, bringing God glory. I went on a limb and spoke, "Let There Be Light," when I couldn't find my sunglasses. In the stillness that followed, I could see them in my mind's eye.

When you speak Light into your situation, your guidance system will engage and the end result will bring glory to God...no matter how long it takes.

Revelation 7:9-10

Acknowledging God for His awesomeness, that's worship. Living in that, orienting your life by that Light, will bring you to your destiny. Trivia, memories, and taking action (speaking Light) are ways to perk up your senses and bring out the childlikeness He adores. I'm sure there are other ways, but for now, this is what I've got.

There will be people jammed around the throne one day who have learned that all of life is worship. They will have figured out how to live life to the fullest by living to bring glory to the Highest.

I can't wait to experience that day! I've been in mobs before, but not one like this. I plan to be right in the thick of it. Shouting along with people *"...from every nation and tribe and people and language, standing in front of the throne and before the Lamb... clothed in white robes and held palm branches in their hands. And they were shouting with a great roar Salvation comes from our God who sits on the throne and from the Lamb"* (Revelation 7:9).

REAL LIFE STORIES

1. Doing The Bangla and The Ghana

Speaking of meeting around the throne, I've done a little traveling over the years and can imagine that we are going to have quite a time when we all worship around the throne.

In 2006 I went on a missions trip to Bangladesh, a small country to the West of India. I went with a group from my local church for a crusade in which myself and a few children from the church were asked to lead a kids meeting. We had a blast and the kids who were there with me are still living with spirits wide open to Jesus.

During the worship time in that crusade, I absolutely went crazy doing "The Bangla." It's a kind of circular group dance that involves swinging one leg at a time in and out with short hops and twists along the way. I'm sure I was entertaining since I'm a bit of a klutz. But it was one of the first times I'd really enjoyed doing something like this. I think what made it so much fun was remembering Revelation 7:9-10. The Bangla isn't for everyone, but it sure is a fun way to worship!

The year before, 2005, I'd gone to Ghana, West Africa, for a teacher-training seminar and a children's crusade. I noticed people there really, and I do mean really, like to dance. They do a kind of chicken dance. I've discovered it looks cool in Ghana, but outside of Ghana, not so much. They also do very organized hanky dances. Guys dance separately from gals and marrieds dance separately from singles. The music is mostly drums, so keeping the rhythm isn't a problem. When I call it a hanky dance, I'm not talking a hanky wave; I mean they made those hankies dance.

The hanky dance, one for guys and one for gals, I videoed and brought back for my kids group to try. My kids liked it so much; I used it in several training situations afterwards. Not only did it spark joy, but also it helped bring generations together. I'll explain how in the next story.

There are signature moves used in corporate worship all over the world that are interesting and engaging. With a little research, this information can be used to add a "Wow!" factor to any kids worship time. And if you're brave, and your church is open, it can really spice up a corporate worship service as well.

2. Hankies and Buckets

Not long after my trips to Ghana and Bangladesh, I went to a church in Kentucky for a kids ministry weekend. It was a more traditional church, meaning they had a certain order of things, but they gave us full rein that weekend to cut loose.

As we prepared praise banners for children to use, we also prepared a basket full of white hankies for the parents and elders to use. We wanted everyone to be waving something. To children the praise banners were familiar and cool; to their parents and elders white hankies brought back a flood of memories from the good ol' days. Our desire wasn't to flaunt new ideas, rather to build a bridge between old and new.

As the service began children swarmed to the front waving their banners and a few were banging on overturned sand buckets. Everyone else was mouthing words and looking around, not sure if something like this was kosher for "big church." That's when the basket of white hankies came to the rescue. Elders were invited to join the fun, using something more familiar, an hanky. The entire congregation looked like it was in motion as white hankies and colorful banners waved in sync with the music. When it was all said and done, we'd all worked up a sweat.

The Holy Spirit began to do things in that room that surprised us all. People got their groove back, shy children came out of their shell, and one child said something to the effect of, "I like church tonight because we get to do stuff too."

When we were exhausted, the pastor stood behind the pulpit and spoke encouragingly to the entire congregation. I'll never forget what he told them. He said, "If I'd have known some Wal-Mart hankies and buckets would have had this affect on you, I'd have bought them for you a long time ago."

That night I'm quite sure the Light of the World was cracking a smile, basking in the glory those hankies and buckets brought Him. Hosanna in the highest!

QUOTES

1--http://www.sparkpeople.com/mypage_public_journal_individual .asp?blog_id=2207114

2--http://livingwithpower.org/amazing-creation-facts/

QUESTIONS

1. On a scale of 1 to 10, what is your worship score? Is a church-only endeavor, or a way of living?

2. Other than bringing the awe back into awesome, and remembering God's goodness, what's your secret to moving from Me Ville to De Light?

3. Into what situations do you need to consider speaking "Let There Be Light?"

FURTHER READING

1. ***Commanding Your Morning*** by Cindy Trimm
   Great for ideas on how to bring your thoughts into alignment, releasing the overcoming power of the Holy Spirit.

2. ***Holy Bible, "Light"***
   Genesis 1:3; Psalm 4:6, 13:3, 18:28, 19:8, 27:1, 43:3, 76:4, 78:14, 89:15, 90:8, 97:11, 119:105, 130; Proverbs 20:27, Isaiah 9:2, 42:6, 50:10, 58:8, 10, 60:19; Luke 2:32, 11:35; John 1:4, 3:19, 21, 8:2, 11:10, 12:46, Acts 9:7, 12:3, 26:18, 26:23; Romans 13:12; 2 Corinthians 4:4, 6; Colossians 1:2, 1 Thessalonians 5:5; 1 Peter 2:9; 1 John 1:5, 7, 2:8, 10; Revelation 21:24, 22:5.

Chapter 13: I WANT TO PRAY GOOD

During a visit to Vienna, Austria many years ago, I was taken to see the Schönbrunn Palace. This is where Mozart performed from a young age and where his music is greatly appreciated. As such, he is immortalized in a painting commissioned by the empress who adored him.

This painting is unusual. No, the eyes don't move, creeping out visitors, but one of Mozart's shoes does. No matter which way you lean when looking at the painting, one of his shoes is always facing you dead on. On one level, it's kinda weird, on another, it's pretty clever.

I think the Bible is a bit like that shoe. No matter which way I'm leaning, it's always pointing right at me. I don't know of any book, thousands of years in the making that's survived, let alone stayed relevant. Indeed, it is one of the most incredible books ever written and in my opinion its depth is beyond any dimension we mere mortals can perceive. It's fit for children, teens, and college grads, the working class, world leaders, Jews, Christians and surprisingly, even Communists refer to it as good poetry.

Learning to use the Word as a prayer guide makes sense and the good news is, it isn't rocket science. Like the sound of that? Me too. After all, God started it, and through nearly a hundred examples left for us, has explained it.

For years I was stymied as I thought prayers had to come from my head and heart, I didn't realize I could use the Word as my prayer guide. Wouldn't that be cheating? Imagine the joy I discovered when praying the Word in a Spirit-led way. It comes out of my mouth sounding Biblical-ish, but not King Jamesy and over time the way verses began to intertwine proved most fascinating.

God's Eternal Word, Spoken By Me

Praying words from the Bible, God's Word, aloud is different from defensive, begging, and reactionary prayer. It tends to be bold, declarative and sometimes even a bit prophetic. It's as if the origins of the Word come through when it's spoken aloud, even in my voice. It is an offensive weapon, pulled for advancing into new territory or holding onto something attained. Praying God's Word can start as a trickle, but the current underlying that trickle is that of Niagara.

According to Scripture, God's word is eternal (Psalm 119:89), an offensive weapon (Ephesians 6:17), and a quick and powerful something that is sharper than any double-sided sword; piercing our very spirit if necessary (Hebrews 4:12). I need this in my life!

I don't know about you, but I don't just want to train children to read the Word, or memorize it for prizes, I want to train them to use it. Couple the eternal Word with their human words, which have the power of life and death (Proverbs 18:21), and there is no telling how expectations, attitudes, conflicts, problems, beliefs, and any other aspect of life can change. Empowering children with this knowledge is life changing.

Have you ever talked to yourself? Abraham did (Genesis 17:17). Maybe you were trying to remember something, or maybe you were working out a situation and couldn't contain it between your ears. There's a reason for that. When your ears are engaged, your brain takes action slightly faster when your eyes are engaged; and this is especially true for auditory learners. This is why expressing our thoughts, negative or positive, can have such a profound impact on our psyche, and why it plays such an important part during childhood development. If our words hold this power, imagine the vaporizing power contained in God's words.

If the Word is going to impact our spheres of influence we need to speak it out of our mouths. God's ears, our ears, and a host of other ears will process it, whether they are my children's ears or ears of the spirit realm tuned to our world. As God's representative on planet Earth, I've been instructed to imitate Christ. He spoke the Word, so I get to do it as well.

Paul described the Word as a sword. Following this analogy, that sword unwielded, unspoken, is about as useful as one lying around in its scabbard. Looking at the sword, thinking about it and admiring it, is not the same as picking it up and swinging it around. Furthermore, swinging it around is not the same as wielding it. Learning to use the Word takes practice, but is easier than you might think. And it will fit in your hands as well as in the hands of those you train.

Premeditated Prayers

In the past decade the idea of praying God's Word has grown from obscurity to popularity. These days it is relatively easy to find motivational prayer books, books with monthly prayer plans, books that highlight actual prayers located in the Bible, and books that give practical how to's for praying Scripture. Some of my favorites and a few new discoveries are listed on the reading list at the end of this chapter for your consideration. If you are new to this idea, or perhaps a little rusty, being educated is a great first step. Using truths you discover along the way, as led by the Holy Spirit, will net you the results you've dreamed of.

As you educate yourself, and do a few trial runs out of curiosity, I'm sure you'll appreciate how nice it is to slow down, perhaps even write down your prayers. It's not quantity, but quality you're building. To me, there is something about putting thought into my prayers as I pray, or even ahead of praying, that makes the process so rewarding.

Children often miss this rewarding feeling of praying the Word, mostly because of the environment we create when training them in this area. Either we amp things up to keep their attention, or we go so low-key they are ready for a snooze. We give too many generalities without instruction or overload them with too many specifics, making the idea too complex to take seriously.

Generally speaking, when do you experience that rewarding feeling? Doesn't it come when you've done something well? If you want children to feel they "pray good," activities that generate a sense of satisfaction and accomplishment, activities that build on their strengths, are worth considering.

Children get a sense of satisfaction and accomplishment when they can track their growth or change. They go to school to learn things about the natural world. They come to you to learn things about the spiritual world. Sometimes methods can overlap between worlds. Children like self-competition, group-competition, rewards, opportunities, and trying new things. Incorporating these elements into a time of premeditated prayer makes it possible for them to get that "rewarding feeling." That rewarding feeling fuels further exploration and curiosity about spiritual life.

From what children have told me, if they can "get good at prayer," then they feel maybe they have a chance to "get good at being a Christian." While this isn't the ultimate goal, being good "Christians," it is a road marker along the way to raising up a generation of children who know how to pray, a generation of children who can wield the sword of the Spirit for the glory of God.

Using The Language Of The Bible

At a children's ministry training weekend, I heard Stacey Campbell suggest the idea that praying in the language of the Bible helps us connect with God. I wasn't sure about it, and to be honest, I sat there a bit skeptically. We did some pretty cool things as a group, praying the Word aloud in a manageable translation (aka non-KJV), but I didn't see the advantage of using the language of the Bible much. I filed the thought for a later time.

Several years later, I stumbled on something for a project I was working on. As it turns out, Stacey was right. When we learn to use the language of the Bible we pick up details about spiritual life that we would otherwise never know, thus impacting our perceptions and understanding of the world. A person's language, whether English, Chinese or "Bible," impacts his worldview.

Why? Research suggests we unconsciously become attentive to things within a language that others who aren't familiar with it wouldn't pick up. These habits of language are cultivated at very young ages; therefore it is never too early to begin introducing children to the language of the Bible. Creating habits of mind that go beyond the Biblical language itself impact everything from experiences, feelings, memories, and even one's place in the world.

So, not only is learning to pray Scripture in a premeditated way beneficial to one's prayer life, absorbing and learning to speak the language of the Bible impacts our life experience. Helping children create habits of mind that lead to a fulfilled life and answered prayers is far more interesting to me than simply teaching a lesson or throwing together a "thought" to share.

As you can see, I've spent a handful of pages demonstrating various ways we can assist children in their hunger to "pray good." There is no one way that will suit every challenge of life, but through the process of education, experimentation, a little language acquisition, and loads of practice, children can get that rewarding feeling to help them deepen and broaden their walk with God.

Backward Compatible

I don't always have the newest tech, but I try not to let it get too far away from me. I just don't like the headache of trying to catch up. I feel the energy expended keeping up is less than the energy it would take to catch up later. I'm not an early adopter, in much of anything, physically or spiritually. I'm sort of the middle person who is teachable and willing to pass on what I've learned. Because of this, I pay attention to something called, backward compatibility. To front runners, it doesn't matter, but to someone like me who is trying to get in on the newest thing (once the bugs are worked out) yet be able to relate with the late adopters, it's important.

I'm so relieved and happy to tell you praying the Word is backward compatible. No matter what version of the Jesus operating system you're running, praying the Word will work. No matter how many years you may have let prayer slide, collecting cobwebs in the junk room, praying the Word will plug right in. As with anything, it takes a little practice for the user to get the hang of it, but praying the Word just works. Plug it in and go. Kind of like an Apple computer. Okay, that was uncalled for.

Born For Bravery

Larissa Hunt is probably one of the most interesting case studies of children who have learned to pray the Word. She is the one who helped coin the phrase, "Premeditated Prayer." I've followed her development from her elementary school years and couldn't be more pleased to share a bit of her story with you.

Larissa, a bit quiet and referred to as, "shy," started praying in group situations at my local church toward the end of her primary school years. She ducked her head and mumbled through most of those early prayers, extremely uncomfortable, but willing to try.

When we began doing Scripture Prayer training using the Shekinah Kids curriculum, she took to it like a duck to water. The first premeditated prayer was written out and slid under her parents door not long after she learned how to use a concordance. Though still in primary school at the time, her prayer brought healing to her mom. Shortly after, another prayer was given to her dad and it was answered with a job. Over time, she continued to use this method to speak her heart and share her faith. Even her grandfather was a beneficiary of her premeditated prayer. She wrote one for him as he lay dying that he would turn back to God. She wasn't disappointed when her grandfather did just that.

Through practice she gained courage and was usually one of the first volunteers when I asked for someone to pray aloud. She was happy to lead in a prayer over the offering in children's church and didn't draw back when invited to pray monthly over the missions offering in "Big Church."

She kept quietly morphing. Eventually it got the attention of church leaders, even a missionary. The change in her family got the attention of CBN. As a result, they were interviewed as part of a piece CBN did on children ministering in the church. By age 14 she had prayed for a crowd of 18,000 young people, sparking similar activities in another nation.

As a child she felt called to work with orphans. This calling was reinforced, fed through a constant diet of related prayer efforts every week for years of kids prayer practices. Just after entering high school she visited an orphanage in Guatemala and determined that helping orphans was indeed her life's path. With a new intensity she began planning her high school and college years accordingly.

Upon arrival in the youth group, Larissa led in prayer by example. Her prayerfulness led to open doors in other areas of involvement that provided training for her life's work. She graduated from high school and moved on to college to get a medical degree, still living in the sweet spot of her potential.

This past Monday night her mom told me she passed one of the most difficult anatomy tests with a B, the highest score in her class. Two years into college and she's still going strong. It's no coincidence. Larissa's habit of premeditated prayer has served her well, bringing much glory to God already in her young life.

She was one brave little girl who is maturing into one brave woman of God. What's even better is she knows it's about God's glory, not her own dreams and plans.

QUESTIONS

1. What interests you most about the idea of praying the Word?

2. How is self-talk different from prayer? Self-talk is the conversation constantly running in your mind that you may or may not verbalize.

3. Are there any habits of mind you have picked up from exposing yourself to the language of the Bible? If so, what are they?

FURTHER READING

1. ***Praying The Bible*** by Wesley & Stacey Campbell
   Full of prayers recorded in the Bible; giving over eighty examples of prayers on various topics. Great for an idea starter.

2. ***Praying God's Word Day By Day*** by Beth Moore
   A compact book with a Scripture prayer for each day of the year. Excellent for getting prayer ideas and building consistency.

3. ***Believing God*** by Beth Moore
   Not only with this book help you pray better, it will challenge you to truly believe the Scriptures concerning your standing with God. Really believing makes for expectant pray-ers.

4. *I Declare* by Joel Osteen

   A 31-day guide to experience the power of the spoken Word of God. Not exactly "prayer," but informs readers about the blessings and benefits of speaking out.

5. ***Change Your Words, Change Your Life*** by Joyce Meyer

   Practical ways to put your thoughts and words on "things above" to impact your daily life. Again, not exactly "prayer," but trains your brain to think right so you can act right, which leads to confidence when you pray.

6. ***www.shekinahkids.com***

   Get more information here about how to motivate and track progress as children learn to pray the Word.

Chapter 14: TILL KINGDOM COME

"May your Kingdom come soon. May your will be done on earth, as it is in heaven" (Matthew 6:10).

We use that phrase, "till kingdom come," to illustrate the idea of forever, as if that day will never arrive. But the truth these days is the Kingdom is a shimmering breath away from sweeping us off our feet. The "till" is no longer stretching out before us. We are in it and pushing right up against its boundaries.

The Kingdom coming is not one of my making. It's solely made by the Creator Himself, for Himself to be shared and enjoyed by us, His Bride, His Children. As such, I have authority in Christ, not to mold His Kingdom in my image, but to allow the Christ in me to join forces with the Christ in others. Together, as we bring Glory to God, that Kingdom gets ever closer to materializing.

It is a supernatural work of the Spirit, this Kingdom building. Our job is to live in a way that makes His name, the name of Jesus, famous among our family, peers, communities...nations. Noah's descendants made the mistake of living to make *their* names famous (Genesis 11:4). They sought to build a kingdom in their image and it didn't sit well with God.

We should take care not to let this history replicate itself in our lives or in the lives of the children we teach. When we join in unity to bring glory to ourselves, we sideline God, and to put it mildly, He doesn't care much for that approach.

The Bible Is A Book Of Missions

I was sitting somewhere around the third row listening with my ears and heart to Esther Ilinsky teach on missions being the central theme of the Bible. She held up a large picture of the Tower of Babel and asked, "What story is this picture about." Our answers told the shallow lesson. But she was looking for something deeper. "What's the point of this story?" She prompted. Quiet and nervous smiles met her steady gaze.

Mama Esther, as her friends know her, explained the story from a new vantage point. God scattered people in order to receive worship from every corner of the globe, which was His intention from the beginning. As proof we need only turn to prophetic writings throughout Scripture. Some day people from the four corners of the earth, of every tribe and tongue will worship God around His throne. He knew what was coming and set the stage for it eons ago. "This story is a story of missions," she said.

She moved on.

Next she held up a large picture showing David hurling his stone at Goliath. "What's the point of this story?" Now everyone was quiet, waiting for her insight. So she asked, "Why did David kill Goliath?" The usual answers came up. He was threatening God's people. David wasn't afraid, etc. We all agreed the point was not that little kids could do great things for God, though it is the tag line many teachers like to use. I've even used it.

We waited.

Esther smiled, eyes sparkling, as she explained to us David told the giant why he was going to kill him. It was another prompt, but none of us remembered that detail. So we looked it up. 1 Samuel 17:46, the last sentence.

Today the LORD will conquer you, and I will kill you and cut off your head. And then I will give the dead bodies of your men to the birds and wild animals, and <u>the whole world will know that there is a God in Israel!</u>

Again, she said it, "This story is a story of missions!" Can you see David's motivation? Was it to make his name famous? Was it to burnish the reputation of Israel? No, on the contrary, he did this courageous, crazy act to make the LORD's name famous!

She wasn't done. She had two more examples to go to make her point clear. At the time, many of the lessons based on Bible stories provided in various curriculums were actually feeding a humanistic hunger in children because they did not focus on God's glory but on a minute detail or "practical application."

The three Hebrew children who wouldn't bow, thrown in the furnace. What's the point? God's name was made famous by their actions to live or die for His glory. Check it out in Daniel 3, especially verse 29.

Final example; that of Daniel himself. When he survived the lions, king Darius made a decree about Daniel's God (Daniel 6:25-27). Daniel's life made God's name famous in the entire known world.

Over time as I began to rethink many of the Bible stories, I started finding similar threads. Then it dawned on me. As I live my life for God's glory, I live a life of missions, and I do this through natural use of my talents (teaching, writing, computer work), making His name famous.

As you pause to reflect on familiar Bible stories, I challenge you to look for the deeper meaning that shows God's glory and makes His name famous. The greatest help we need concerns how to live life in a way that makes God famous.

15 ~~Minutes~~ Seconds of Fame

American Idol. It's a TV show chronicling the rise of people hoping to become famous through singing. Something about the title feels a little cockeyed to me, but I've seen the tryouts, and nearly laughed myself silly. It is amazing to me what some people are willing to do for a few moments of fame. Having survived nine seasons, copycat shows are mushrooming. Shows like, The Voice, X Factor, and America's Got Talent, just to name a few, have cropped up.

We seem to be feeding a national hunger for attention with something akin to spiritual junk food. Isn't this yet another trend entertaining us away from God?

If so, how do we refocus children's attention to help them think about making God's name famous? We begin to emphasize it a thousand different ways. When everyone else is focused on self-promotion is there a way to foster David-like responses? We train them to live for God's glory. And when it seems everyone else is concerned about fitting in, how do we train children to stand out as the four Hebrew boys did so long ago? We shift from a "Me-Ology" theology to a "Thee-Ology" theology.

Me-Ology vs. Thee-Ology

Moving away from a Me-Ology to a Thee-Ology in simple terms, means shifting the focus from what we want to what God wants. And I'll give you a clue. What God wants is glory.

Me-Ology is a way to depict a *religion* in which God's primary concern should be to make me happy; it tells the story of me and mine. Thee-Ology depicts an *experience*, a relationship actually, wherein my primary concern is to bring God glory. By making our lives, down to our very prayers about bringing God glory; it keeps Him ever in our thoughts and vision. It draws us closer to Him as such a lifestyle brings Him great delight.

One of the problems with Me-Ology is it promotes something of an "A-List Mentality." The hidden message is that everyone should do something BIG for God. This idea is backed up with story after story illustrating a "famous" character and his or her awe-inspiring actions. While these stories are good, a steady diet of them has the reverse effect from what one might expect. As a result, some children end up spending a lot of time wondering what BIG thing *they* can do *for* God, which feeds the "me" in Me-Ology. Other children don't bother because they have little hope in *themselves* of ever reaching such heights; again feeding the "me" in Me-Ology.

Making the transition is certainly worth the effort. Just last week a proud parent told me of the actions of his daughter that brought God glory. The concept of hearing God's voice and obeying has served as a strong foundation for her; now she's building on it.

As the story goes, last year she felt to pledge $50 per month for a special missions project. She couldn't look to her family for the money, and as a high school student without a job, she had no idea where the funds would come from. Soon after, she got a job and worked hard and faithfully at it. Day-by-day, week-by-week she worked to make her pledge and never missed a payment. Having fully paid her pledge, she's a step closer to understanding money is never an issue with God.

In her case, God didn't send her a cashier's check or money order. She didn't win the lottery as a result of her willingness to make the pledge. It's nice when God supplies miraculously. But this time, what she did took obedience, commitment and a kind of theology that went beyond an incomplete God-view. She has transitioned, at least in this area of her life, to Thee-Ology.

A Thee-Ology mindset gets excited contemplating Genesis 1:1-25; all the stuff God did before He created us. Someone with a Thee-Ology God-view knows it's okay for some to do great things while others faithfully do things tagged as mundane. A Thee-Ology perspective means someone has taken time to dive into the deep of God and emerge with a priceless pearl.

Think for a moment with me. Which would you subscribe to on most days? Me-Ology or Thee-Ology? Which God-view does your teaching and training most reflect?

Perhaps you are like me? A mixture of both types. But I like to think one side is outweighing the other. Which one is that? The one that focuses most on God.

Take a look at a few common misconceptions to see what the Word has to say about them. If you side with the Word, try them on your children to see how they fare.

> Why did Christ die on the cross? To save me from hell, or to bring glory to God (John 17:4)?

> Why does God heal? Because someone I care about or know is sick, or to bring glory to His name (John 11:4)?

The way to get a generation to live and pray in alignment with what God wants is to teach them to hear His voice, give them an opportunity to obey, and let them understand their lives (talents and dreams) and prayers are to make God famous.

To further study this idea of Me-Ology and Thee-Ology, pick up a copy of the book, *Cat & Dog Theology*. It's a great resource and will challenge you in more ways than you can imagine. It is also a great series of lessons that can be adapted for children.

Alignment

I'm sure you've wondered as you've read the word "alignment" previously what I was referring to, "exactly." It's a very simple concept but only possible when a person begins holding more Thee-Ology positions than Me-Ology ones. Therefore, it seemed logical to me to write about it here.

When you or I live life revolving around God, bringing Him glory is a natural result. Delight is in the picture too, making it even sweeter. Not easier, just better. Alignment is what occurs when we center our lives around God with consistency, over and over, day in and day out. Little things, big things, medium things, long things, short things; all done in a way that circles God. It's when you notice Me-Ology is left in the dust of yesterday and Thee-Ology is always on your mind.

Living in alignment is what makes it possible to pray, "Let Your kingdom come! Do down here as You see it up there." If you're out of alignment, the last thing you will want to ask for is His kingdom to come. And without alignment, you'll be scared to death to permit God to work in your life the way He has seen it since the time before your birth. Alignment comes with a Thee-Ology mindset and is a frustration for those living under the constraints of Me-Ology.

Balance

When talking about spiritual things, the word "balance," can be a sticky subject. On the one hand, Jesus pretty well let it be known that life with Him is an all or nothing pursuit, which leaves little room for the idea of balance. On the other hand, there is a valid concern by leaders and parents that children, left to their own devices will go too far, leaving Spirit-led prayer behind for that of their own emotions. The key here is, "left to their own devices."

As you train children in Spirit-led prayer, you will yourself need to get into the habit of listening first before you pray so it will feel natural, not stilted to your children. In time, you want your habit of "listen first, petition later" to rub off on your children. Asking God to direct you to pray in a way that maximizes His glory is a healthy way to grow the habit.

This simple step of listening first is incredibly important, especially in the area of intercession. As you may have experienced or witnessed, intercession can take a person to a very deep, emotional place where prayer is more like groaning. While the Apostle Paul wrote about this experience as a good thing, leaving children unattended in this state is never a good idea.

In their immaturity, they may miss the point where Spirit-led prayer stops and emotions take over. They will need your help to safely disconnect and learn where that line between the Holy Spirit and human emotion is.

If you are around children and suspect this transition from Holy Spirit to human emotion occurs, simply get their attention, and redirect them to either stop praying, or have a conversation with them about why they are praying the way they are. This is how they will learn and how you open yourself up to be led by the Holy Spirit as well. If you sense they are Spirit-led let it go.

If you are unsure, but feel you should redirect them, their reaction to your prompt will confirm whether they are in the Spirit or doing their own thing. If anything rises up in them against you, you can pretty much know they were digging into their own human emotion.

This reminds me of something I saw just this weekend. It illustrates my point and also demonstrates how posture and body language are indicators of what's going on inside a child.

During a prayer time, children had been standing, heads back, hands raised praying for others and there was a great move of God. Some of the children, who were not yet Spirit-filled, came and knelt down, buried their heads in their hands and began to cry. After several minutes of this, some of the Spirit-filled children began to pray with them. The mood in the room shifted. It was a palpable change.

One of the speakers, a Children's Pastor, took the mic and encouraged everyone to stand up and raise their faces and hands again. The mood lifted, and the Holy Spirit began stirring in our midst again. Without that prompt, human emotion would have squelched what the Holy Spirit was trying to do. They needed a little guidance, a little balance, to help them reach for new heights.

Just as with anything else, as children mature, they can experience more and dig deeper. All will be safe and in order as long as they learn where the line between the Holy Spirit and human emotion is. Children left to their own devices, without training, will walk out of balance, not experiencing God's fullest delight because they will have the habit of being led by their emotions instead of God's Spirit.

Put Your Life Where Your Mouth Is

If you're ready to take being Spirit-led to the next level, then this bit is for you. I heard a missionary once say, "If you aren't willing to be part of the solution, don't pray the prayer." Wow! That left a mark.

Over the past twenty-something years, much prayer has been sent up for people living in the 10/40 Window, and I am pretty sure in the years ahead, prayers will continue to rise for needs there and beyond. The Body of Christ has gotten organized and in many places, educated on strategic prayer needs around the world.

Missions mobilizers spread stories of children and teens that have raised funds for water projects, churches, orphanages, and various other needs in emerging and third world nations. Word has spread of church groups, Sunday school classes and individuals who sponsor orphans, support missionaries, send money to rescue slaves or build schools. I even know of some who plan their life of service from an early age.

When children begin praying for all the various needs, some needs will call out to them louder than others. This is a way the Holy Spirit is inviting them on a joint venture. Expect this in your children and encourage it from a "Thee-Ology," standpoint. The focus is to bring God glory, to make His name great. As children live to make God's name famous, they will live a life of missions of some kind.

Get ready to give to mission trips for teens. Get ready to plan a trip to a nursing home or perhaps somewhere overseas. Get ready to have your life changed as God works through you to make His name famous to your children!

REAL LIFE STORIES

1. Adrian's Transformation

I met Adrian during a Kids Prayer weekend in Colorado. He was a lively nine-year-old, so he had my attention. I watched him and was touched at his reaction to praying for people in the 10/40 Window. He cried puddles over his handful of M&Ms. Not only that, but he paid attention and participated at every turn. I found out his mother had been praying God would use that weekend to change his life.

Fast-forward six years to September 2011. Adrian was the youth voice that opened a large national conference with prayer. I got to hear his prayer streaming online and was so proud.

Thanks to a mother's prayer and a family's support, this young man is learning to live life in a way that makes God famous, "till Kingdom come." I can't wait to see where his road leads!

Adrian 2005   **Adrian 2011**

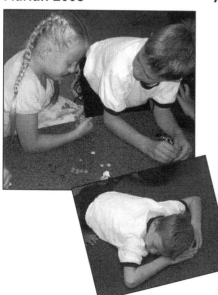

2. Botswana Prayer Wall

During a kids prayer camp in Botswana, after doing a session on the 10/40 Window, I spoke about putting other's needs ahead of my own and encouraged the children to try it. It was a simple request with a simple story, so I was curious to see how it would be received.

Immediately after giving my spiel, I drew their attention to a long white banner at the back of the room on the wall. I then asked children to go and write five requests each on the banner. To my surprise, there was not one personal request. All of the requests were for something 10/40 related or for something outside of personal needs (including immediate family members).

They got it...and got it quick. We had an incredible prayer time following as children wandered here and there on the wall, praying for others every step of the way.

QUESTIONS

1. How is contemplating the Bible as a book of missions beneficial in leading children in Kingdom Praying?

2. How do your children feel about the idea of living to make God's name famous? How well do they understand the idea of bringing God glory?

3. How does a Me-Ology Christian transition to a Thee-Ology Christian?

4. How often do you check for personal alignment with the Holy Spirit? What are the pros and cons of this practice?

5. If you run a children's prayer ministry already, or if you are nurturing children in intercession, how balanced is your group?

6. What steps are you taking now to put your life where your prayers are?

FURTHER READING

1. ***www.operationworld.org***
   Full of motivational resources, this website contains information that is great for prayer and food for thought.

2. ***www.win1040.com***
   This website offers a guide for a systematic approach to praying for 10/40 Window nations.

3. ***You Can Change The World Volume 2*** by Daphne Spraggett, Jill and Patrick Johnstone
   This is an awesome book for children to use when praying for unreached people groups or for 10/40 Window nations. Full of colorful illustrations, prayer points and background information, it's a must-have educational tool

4. ***Window On The World*** by Daphne Spraggett and Jill Johnstone
   Like the previous book, this one provides prayer points and information, but does so with photographs instead of illustrations. Designed for slightly older children, there are more groups listed in the book and more ideas about how to pray for them.

5. ***The Hole In Our Gospel*** by Richard Stearns
   Written by the CEO of World Vision, a non-profit humanitarian agency, this book examines the misconceptions we have about "missions" and challenges readers to invest in "crazy obedience."

Chapter 15: POINT OF CONTACT

I like to think if I'd been around when Jesus was walking the dusty roads in Israel, we would have been friends. At the very least, I can imagine being part of the crowds that clamored to touch or be touched by Him. From what I read, people of all walks of life, even children, were attracted to Him. Sometimes it makes me wish I could travel back in time to have been there too.

I like to be around people who connect with others well through words and deeds, and what better person was there at it than Jesus? He had a corner on the market of changing lives with His life. I wouldn't trade my relationship now, but there are times I'd like to experience being around Jesus…with skin.

The desperate woman who elbowed her way toward His feet to touch the hem of His clothes, healed. The ten lepers surprised when Jesus stopped to touch the untouchables, healed and one made whole. For some with an uncanny understanding of Kingdom dynamics, His words of deliverance were touch enough to heal loved ones far away. It seems wherever Jesus was, people were drawn to Him; wanting to experience something of His touch.

And then it was time for Jesus to leave. Can you imagine the pain that shot through His disciples as they watched Him ascend in the clouds? Having made it past the agony of the cross, having celebrated the resurrection and having spent time in close proximity since, watching Him go must have been one part amazing and two parts pure heartbreak. Realizing they would never again see the twinkle in His eye or feel a love pat as He walked past must have nearly gutted them.

But, Jesus thought of everything and that day a plan made from the foundation of the world was activated that is still in force to this day. His plan was to put His spirit in them, to be with them in that way through the rest of their lives. The good news is there has been and still is enough of Jesus to be poured out into every hurting soul.

When Jesus ascended, though His glorified body left the earth, He didn't desert mankind. Within days, the world began to realize the gift of Himself, now called "The Comforter," alive in each born again, Spirit-filled believer. His Body, the "Body of Christ," was indeed alive and active on planet earth. According to things recorded in the Book of Acts people were drawn to this new Body in droves. Where once people were drawn to Jesus, they were now drawn by that same Spirit to His Body left here to continue His work.

It didn't matter that the face wasn't the same, what mattered was the Spirit was the same. As the spirit of Jesus filled believers they began to do the same works He did when He was here physically. Miracles took place. Healing, deliverance, and spiritual gifts from another realm were released to work in His global body. What a brilliant plan!

In Acts chapter 5 people recognized the spirit of Jesus in Peter. So desperate for a touch, they laid friends and family in the streets so that as Peter's very shadow touched them, they were instantly healed by the same power of God that flowed through Jesus. I can't explain that except to think of how Jesus told His disciples they would do greater things (John 14:12).

I'm not inferring people should be healed when you or I pass by them in a parking lot. What I'm hoping to demonstrate is how the same Spirit that made Jesus the Christ, is the same Spirit that makes me a teacher and you a whatever-it-is-you-are. That spirit of Jesus in me attracts people who need His touch through me. People attracted to the spirit of Jesus in you need His touch through you. People are also attracted to the spirit of Jesus in your children and need their touch.

Let's take this a step further. People who need what I have through the power of the Holy Spirit are drawn to me. People who need what you have through the power of the Holy Spirit are not drawn to me, but to you. You are the face on the spirit of Jesus to those in your world. Wow! What a thought. The gifts and abilities built into your spirit make it possible to touch people in a way that heals and sets free, if you believe. If.

Unfortunately for many Christians, they believe they can be saved through the work of Jesus on the cross, but they don't believe having His spirit in them draws people to them for a Kingdom purpose. Many preachers preach salvation and a Spirit-filled life, but leave out the element of touching others the way Jesus touched...with compassion and power to heal and deliver.

As long as there is a Body of Christ globally present, people will continue to be drawn to Jesus. In this way, people haven't changed much in 2000 years. However, when we, who are filled with the spirit of Jesus don't see with compassion and don't touch with power, well, it means there is a disconnect in the Body. Synapses are firing—the Holy Spirit is speaking direction—but, the messages are getting scrambled—incomplete teachings from man's wisdom—or not being delivered at all—silence on teaching in this area.

I think you're getting the idea. I'm not only referring to physical healing here. Jesus touched and spoke with emotionally damaged people, making them whole. Think of the Sycharian woman at the well (John 4:6-30), the adulterous woman thrown to His feet (John 8:3-11), and the demon possessed Gadarene (Luke 8:36) for starters. After the cross, even Peter could fall into this category. After his treacherous denial of Jesus an angel at the tomb specifically named him to be told of Jesus' resurrection (Mark 16:7). Those words to Peter were no doubt healing ones.

I know what it is to be drawn to Jesus. I know what it is to be touched by Him mystically—those tingles on my spine—and physically—those words and actions of people filled with His Spirit. I know what it is to be healed emotionally and physically; I'm talking broken heart and a broken bone. I know well what it is to receive. I hunger to be one who is increasingly adept at giving.

I'm hoping you too know some of this from personal experience, both the receiving and giving of healing. I'm hoping you'll find a way to share this in bite-sized nuggets with your children. As a part of the Body of Christ on earth, we are led to pray for, minister to, and touch others; it's what Jesus does, therefore, it is what we, His Body, does. Learning how to participate in this paradigm takes practice and the firing synapses from the mind of Christ to direct my spirit.

Led To Pray For Others

As someone with an independent streak, I must say, learning to be led by an invisible whisper has not been easy. Perhaps one of the biggest pitfalls was the question, "Was that God or me?" I've learned though it's a valid question, it's also a stalling technique, a weapon in the hands of the enemy. I try to cancel it by applying two things easy to remember.

First, I replay Isaiah 54:17 through my head.

> *"But in that coming day <u>no weapon turned against you will</u> <u>succeed. You will silence every voice raised up to accuse</u>*

you [even if it is my own]. These benefits are enjoyed by the servants of the Lord; their vindication will come from me. I, the Lord, have spoken (Isaiah 54:17, emphasis mine).

Second, I apply this bit of logic. If what I feel or hear to do is good and won't hurt anyone, I do it. If it wasn't God, then perhaps He is rubbing off on me since I thought to do something good. If it may hurt someone or myself, I pause or wait to make sure. If it contradicts the Word or goes against what I know is right, I reject it.

I want it to be first nature, not second, to walk as I'm led. Some of being led comes from what I know and can confirm, and some comes from what I hear as I wait on God.

Recently at lunch with a few close friends, I was reminded that people can "hear" from God in different ways. As my buddies exchanged stories, I realized their way of "hearing God" is much different from me. Unlike them, I don't "see" things often, but I "feel" things in my spirit. As I've led children in this area over the years, I've learned to pay attention to what I feel and I'm pretty sure that was a divine set up.

You see, I didn't always pay attention to my feelings. For many years I used denial and other methods to push away feelings I didn't like or understand. Knowing this is a way God speaks to me has radically changed the way I deal with my feelings. I don't understand everything, but I at least pay attention to them and filter them through His Word.

So, when it comes to feelings, how do I proceed? The strong feelings are me, the quiet ones are God. The screaming in my head is me, the quiet whisper floating past is usually God. The bright idea? Me. The God idea niggling the back of my mind? The one I'm prone to ignore? That's God, every single time.

As for the feelings others try to project on me from their own life, I'm getting better at catching them before they enter to confuse me. Until a few years ago, I didn't realize it was possible to project feelings onto others. I find it happens in relationships more than we might suspect and it makes the idea of putting on the breastplate and helmet very appealing to me.

We are led by seeing or hearing or feeling to pray for others. We are led, as people are attracted to the spirit of Jesus in us. Knowing how to pray requires listening with our physical and spiritual ears. Sometimes we don't need to focus on the obvious, but on the root problem beneath the surface. Knowing how to do that requires listening and a spark of faith that looks to God's glory and not to human wishes, hopes or understanding.

Tapping Into God's Glory

Job's life brought God much glory...and brought Job much pain and questions. We see in the end how it all worked out for Job, but that isn't God's formula for all of us. That was His formula for Job. Looking back on Job's experience, of course we learn much about God and the workings of the heavenlies. But to make Job the template for how God handles my life is dangerous thinking, and teaching such is dangerous teaching. (Yes, I ate my protein bar this morning; I know that was a bit strong.) It's dangerous because sometimes the hero dies when we would least expect it or in a way we can't accept. Sometimes God gets glory from a life in a way that seems absolutely preposterous from our puny perspective.

So, how do we pray for someone at death's door or someone classified as terminally ill? The same way we would pray for any other person: listen first, ask, build faith, and be bold. In any situation, listen to what the Holy Spirit is saying. If directed to interject a prophetic word into the situation, interject it. If directed to express compassion, express it. If directed to speak peace into turmoil, speak it. Seek God's glory in any given prayer opportunity, even for healing. And if necessary, pray again…and again.

Once Isn't Always Enough

Have you prayed for someone who was expecting healing and they had only a slight improvement? Does that mean your prayers didn't work? Does that mean it's time to quit? Not usually. If the Holy Spirit says pray for healing, then keep on praying. If the Holy Spirit says otherwise, pray the "otherwise."

The best example I know to cite here is one recorded in Mark 8 where Jesus spit into a blind man's eyes. Does that count as "touch?" I think I would have jumped back if it had been me. With this first "touch" the man could see a bit, but it wasn't enough. So Jesus put his hands on the man's eyes "again," and his eyes were opened.

If Jesus touched "again" for someone, why on earth would I be snookered into believing it wouldn't happen to me? Why would I stop short, discouraged? Why should I expect to be a one-prayer wonder? It's safe to say every prayer Jesus prayed was answered, and it's good to realize not every prayer He prayed was a Lazarus-come-forth prayer. I don't know how this affects you, but whenever I stop to reconsider this truth, my spirit sighs a sigh of relief.

In Chapter 6, story three is from Bridgeton, Missouri. A Sunday school teacher's ear was healed one Sunday when children commanded her ear to hear in the name of Jesus. Children did not go into intercession over her ear. They spoke to it, saying, "Ear!

Hear! In Jesus' name!" over and over. That prayer was actually a multi-step process.

It went like this. After the first burst of faith, her pain was gone, but she still couldn't hear. So her students prayed again, commanding the ear to hear. The pain was still gone, and she could hear a little. She wouldn't settle and neither would the children. So they prayed again. The third time, her ear popped and her hearing returned to normal. We all went home psyched!

The Thing About Pain

I am not the only one to discover this, but when praying for healing, pain is usually the first thing to go or dissipate. Its departure builds faith if it is necessary to pray again. But it is important to remember, pain is only a symptom of a problem. When it leaves, if the root problem persists, the pain very likely will come back. This is why sometimes you will feel you need more information to pray specifically. If this happens don't be afraid to stop and get more information from the person you're praying for or from the Holy Spirit.

Another thing about pain is, sometimes people don't really want to be healed. So no matter how much faith you have, if they're not in on it with you, you're setting yourself up for a disappointment.

I heard an evangelist once talk about laying hands on a deaf person who didn't want to be healed. As God's power flowed, the man resisted and shook his head, "No!" Seeing such a strong reaction, the evangelist moved on to someone else. The story goes, the deaf man was afraid of how drastically his life would change and his benefits drop if he entered the hearing world. He resisted being healed. What did the evangelist do? Knowing God is the Healer, he simply moved on to the next person.

Sometimes pain is a part of a person's identity or perhaps a person is so accustomed to their pain they don't feel it anymore. These are just a few additional reasons why it's important to be Spirit-led when we pray for someone's healing. Just because you see a deaf person or someone in a wheelchair, it doesn't mean it's a visual cue to start rebuking, laying on hands and commanding. Following the L.A.B.B. Method works in just about every situation. Listen, ask, build faith and be bold.

Some nine pages after beginning this chapter, I hope you understand that it's you and I who are the point of contact for those drawn to Christ. His spirit within us continues to attract people who need His touch. My prayer is He will use my touch and yours to meet those needs.

REAL LIFE STORIES

1. Wall Of Weird Material

The spunky, if imaginary, Smallville High School journalist, Chloe Sullivan, kept a Wall of Weird in her journalism room on campus. On this wall she posted strange stories that made the local paper. This story is one that would definitely have caught her eye and might have even made it to that wall. I don't give any explanation for the story you're about to read, I'm just sharing it because it is absolutely the weirdest thing I've encountered to date.

While holding a children's event in a well-established old church, the pews were loaded with well-established saints. They were great. They danced and prayed right along with the children. When it was time to introduce the L.A.B.B. Method, children were excited but those well-established saints seemed to be holding their collective breath.

When it was time to demonstrate how to walk through the steps in real life, a volunteer stepped forward; let's call her Cheryl. She asked for healing in her knees. As the little seven-year-old walked through the steps of the L.A.B.B. Method, she got stuck on letter A. As the girl asked what to pray for again, the woman confessed she was blind in her left eye, which was a surprise to everyone there. She then mentioned a problem with her feet. That little girl had a tall order, but she began to build faith.

When she felt confident enough to get bold, she started her prayer. Everyone listened intently as the girl zeroed in on Cheryl's eye. After prayer, there was no change. So I felt to ask for an elder to come along side this girl and pray again with her. A volunteer popped right up and came to stand behind Cheryl; lets call her Janice. When the prayer started, Janice placed her hand on Cheryl's shoulder and after a few words from the little girl started to do a jig.

As the girl continued to pray for healing in the eye, Janice continued to jump around as she held onto Cheryl's shoulder. When the prayer ended there was still no change in Cheryl's condition, but Janice's left eye was healed. She could read without her glasses.

Intrigued, but listening intently, I felt to invite another elder to join our little group at the front. Up popped another one who came to stand behind Janice, making what looked like a chain; let's call her Mary. As the little girl prayed again, she focused on the problem with knees. Janice started bucking and newcomer Mary did the same. After the prayer stopped, there was still no change in Cheryl, but Janice could see clearly, and Mary had been healed of back and knee problems. By this time Cheryl, the volunteer, was looking a bit miffed that the healing had seemingly passed through her body into others.

We prayed one more time, and this time everyone got involved. That little girl prayed for Cheryl's feet that the pain would go away. It's as if she instinctively knew to target pain. At the end of the prayer, Cheryl's pain was much less but it seemed she was ready to stop. So we gave God praise for this unusual demonstration and moved on.

That same night, the little girl dreamed of a blue man lying in a bed in a dark hospital room. As she approached him, she knew she had to pray for him. When she did, his normal skin color returned. From this and the events of the previous day, she understood God wanted her to learn to help people in this way. Within a few hours of waking up, her first practical application of this call presented itself and she didn't shy away.

A rowdy boy fell ill suddenly after the morning service so his dad brought him over to me. I called for the little girl to come and pray. Without hesitation she worked through the L.A.B.B. Method and within moments, the boy was fine. When I complimented her, she responded, "I just did what you said and it works."

I know that's a weird story and I'm tempted to "select and delete." But what I know is God got glory that day, and a little girl began walking the path toward her destiny. We won't always be able to sort things, but when we obey, God gets *all* the glory. As a friend of mine says, "There's no way I could think to make something like this up."

2. Raised From The Dead

In the Central America Region children are being taught and trained in spiritual development. It is interesting to me that in this atmosphere of training and practice, God is getting much glory from children who pray. Similar manifestations of God's glory are being reported from Asia as children use what they are learning.

Below is an excerpt of the actual email sent from Missionary Nix in Nicaragua to the regional children's ministries coordinator.

"During the week of prayer and fasting for children in the country of Nicaragua, God used children mightily in Juigalpa. Our district supervisor...reports that four children were at a lady's house by the name of Georgia, when she had a sudden heart attack and fell down to the floor and died. This lady had formerly been a witch, but had been converted and baptized in Jesus' Name! However, she had grown cold and backslidden. Cristóbal and his 3 friends were deeply moved at what they witnessed, and with the faith and sincerity of children, they fell to their knees and began to plead with God. They wept, laid hands on her, and prayed "God, give her another chance." She had been dead about an hour, but they continued to pray. Then suddenly, she was raised back to life again."

QUESTIONS

1. What about you does God use to draw people to Jesus today?

2. When Jesus ascended His physical body left the earth. After that, what of Himself did He give the world? How does that impact lives today?

3. How often do you argue with yourself about doing something God prompts you to do, wondering if it was Him speaking?

4. How should living to bring God glory impact how we speak, touch and pray for others?

5. Should you pray more than once for someone's pain to leave? What do you think is the difference in praying for healing, versus praying for wholeness?

FURTHER READING

1. **Love Out Loud** by Joyce Meyer
   365 daily devotions to help you love God, love yourself and love others. Absorbing this information in daily bite-sized doses will help you touch others from a positive position.

2. **The Me I Want To Be** by John Ortberg
   Understanding that "God wants to redeem you, not exchange, you" is a powerful underpinning for training and ministering (touching) to others.

Chapter 16: COVERAGE

As we collectively and individually work on earth as part of the Body of Christ in this age, spiritual forces and sin challenge us on a daily basis. Spirits governing nations, emerging ideologies and false religions challenge the global Church. Lesser but perhaps no less aggressive spirits governing states, provinces, cities, and municipalities challenge the local church. And lesser yet diabolical spirits seek to infiltrate and sabotage God's plan on a very personal in-your-face level.

When it is all said and done, God has a plan for a thousand years of global domination and administration before He takes the wraps off eternity. But with such a relentless onslaught from every perceivable and unperceivable spiritual deviant, there are times I sometimes wonder how the Body of Christ will make it. Then I am reminded it is through prayer and spiritual renewing that we have arrived at this point in history. It will be by His voice and power that His Body on earth (us) will join the One riding a white horse for a victorious second coming. I anticipate the thrill of that moment; being a united Body, one with Christ Himself.

At the time of this writing, it appears we may have a little time before that last trump sounds (1 Corinthians 15:52; Revelation 10:7, 11:15). In the meantime, I continue training and learning to protect myself spiritually because the intensity of spiritual warfare is coming to a boil; and I don't want to be like the proverbial frog, boiled alive unaware.

Bushwhacked

I have a cousin who loved, and I do mean loved, jumping out from behind a piece of furniture or a wall to scare people. He was good at it too. His kind of ambush was playful, if somewhat irritating. If you swing the pendulum in the other direction from playful to sinister, ambushed morphs into bushwhacked. I have a picture in mind. Think Rwanda, circa late 20th century where family member turned against family member committing unfathomable atrocities. Bushwhacked. Their entire nation was bushwhacked.

In Paul's epistle to the Ephesian church, he spent a considerable amount of time trying to help the church avoid being bushwhacked by selfish living and relational issues (Ephesians 5:1-6:9). He dealt considerably with relationships; relationships between husband and wife, parents and children, and masters and slaves.

Immediately after this detailed relationship advice, Paul in Ephesians 6:10 reminds his readers they do not fight against people. Paul's segue into protecting the Body started with relationships. In essence Paul seems to be saying, handle your relationships so you can face the enemy head on, to avoid getting ambushed in spiritual guerilla warfare.

The enemy comes against us head on with fiery darts, but as with any adversary worth his salt, he looks for a chink in the armor, or a "tell;" something we do out of habit that gives him a clue about our mental or spiritual state. Evil spirits can't read minds, but they have been reading tells like bitterness, unforgiveness, and strife for eons. Many times full blown warfare is averted due to a chink in someone's armor. There are times when just playing off the way a person thinks about himself and handles his relationships are ammo enough.

Why should my enemy waste a fiery dart on me if he can influence someone close to me to jab, jab…jab my kidneys and bust my chops? Why should he be worried about me being a threat if I constantly let my guard down? If I'm clueless about how to protect myself, or what to protect, it's not really warfare anymore is it? It's more like stealing candy from a baby. Now, there might be a whole lot of screaming done by that baby, but nothing will change until that baby grows up and learns to protect itself.

We Ain't Seen Nothin' Yet

I can't resist the urge to go a little Sci-Fi on you. So here it is. I realize I am not enough of a Kingdom mover and shaker to merit the attention of the great dragon, the Devil. It's not my calling and I'm good with that. However, there is a part I can play in his incremental demise as mentioned in Revelation 12:7-12. You might want to take a look at that verse before proceeding, because it applies to you too.

Many people think this falling down of the Devil and his angels refers to something that happens after the rapture of the Church, or something that happened in Genesis. However, in context of verse 11 it seems clear to me we saints are still here when this event takes place. Curious? Go take a peek real quick and come back.

In light of this, I don't train to fight the dragon, that's a job for Michael and his angels. I train that I might through the blood of the Lamb and the word of my testimony be a part of those who participate in bringing him and his minions down. Down from their perch of daily accusation before the throne. When those yahoos are finally gone from the heavenlies, the heavens themselves and those in the heavens will rejoice (Revelation 12:10). Those of us on earth, not so much.

What concerns me a bit is he and his angels will be cast *down.* Down toward our air space and...us. The Scripture prophesies they will be cast to the earth, no longer able to roam the heavenlies freely. Revelation 12:12 warns, *"But terror will come on the earth and the sea, for the devil has come down to you in great anger, knowing that he has little time."*

If you think things are bad now, wait until heaven's furious fallen hosts are jammed into our atmosphere. Things will get even crazier. If we are going to keep it together, we have to learn to apply valuable truths about warfare now. And we have to learn how to get these truths deep into the hearts of our children.

I've had a small taste of it, the acrid assault of hell. As a child I saw demon possession first-hand and all these years later, those experiences have impacted my understanding of the reality of spiritual life. I've seen demonic anger and trust me it isn't pretty. It's spews fiery darts that rip through flimsy faith, piercing unprotected hearts and minds.

Now is the time to hone our skills of listening and obeying. Now is the time to learn to protect our truth receptors, our heart, our mind, our faith, and our salvation. We do this best when we are clearheaded, walking in the light and paying attention.

Clearheaded And Protected

According to the detail of Ephesians 6, in brief what areas need to be protected?

1. Our internal "Truth-o-meter." Our sense of what truth is needs to be calibrated by the Word and not the changing standards of the world around us.

2. Our heart. From which flows love born of the right standing we enjoy with God and others.

3. Our mind. Prepared through peace to be free to share the gospel.

4. Our faith. Used to protect our heart and mind from the direct attacks of the enemy.

5. Our salvation. From which flows our confidence to wield the Sword of the Spirit, which is the Word of God.

Interesting to me is Paul's statement to the Corinthian church in one of his letters. He uses the same thought of not fighting against flesh and blood, but he says it this way,

"We are human, but we don't wage war as humans do. We use God's mighty weapons, not worldly weapons, to knock down the strongholds of human reasoning and to destroy false arguments. We destroy every proud obstacle that keeps people from knowing God. We capture their rebellious thoughts and teach them to obey Christ" (2 Corinthians 10:3-5, emphasis mine).

As you train your children to develop spiritually, I pray you have insight like that of Paul to knock down strongholds of human reasoning and destroy false arguments. I pray you are able to point them to illustrations that will be relevant enough to capture their thoughts, teaching them to obey Christ! You are a part of a Body destined to be clear headed and protected by the armor of faith, love and salvation (1 Thessalonians 5:4-8).

One Size Doesn't Fit All

Now that you're itching to do a series of lessons on living clearheaded and protected, let me meekly suggest you consider cross training in this area. It's true we all need to protect these five general areas (truth, heart, mind, faith and salvation), but how we apply this protection depends largely on our spiritual giftings.

Children need to be aware that they have giftings that go along with their personality. It's been an interest of mine over the years to keep an eye on former students as they mature from toddlers to adults. I've discovered I can expect a child's personality to be set before he exits preschool.

Through primary, middle and high school a child will likely repeatedly face the same challenges, and perhaps even exhibit the same behaviors up through college. Learning how to face those challenges are a part of life's journey. Unless a child learns to put on the armor of God, apply the principals to his life, there is a good chance some of the same challenges that got him in trouble in pre-adolescence will follow him to the grave.

This lets me know I don't need to wait to train young children concerning their giftings. I don't need to wait to explain as the Holy Spirit enlightens me how giftings need to be protected. Children are who they are, and the sooner they recognize their place in the Body of Christ, the sooner they will participate. The sooner they participate, the longer they have to delight in God.

Modified behavior, proper dealings in relationships, and the fruit of the Spirit are just a few indicators of armor being applied. Every personality has its yin and yang, it's pros and cons. Protection comes through shared information, the power of the Holy Spirit, the ministry of deliverance, and personal prayer.

Young David was accustomed to whirling his sling and stones at threats to his sheep. He was adept at grappling with lions and bears with his hands. Yet when he came to the king, he was pressured to wear the king's armor. He politely obliged, but had the sense to recognize the king's armor didn't fit. I applaud David for not only recognizing the snafu, but for calling it out. Standing his ground, he was allowed to serve using weapons with which he felt most familiar, king's armor aside.

Do your children and others a favor. Be careful not to repeat king Saul's mistake. Just because some spiritual discipline, protective maneuver, or offensive stance works well for you, don't force it on everyone else. Explore it and share it, but don't expect it to be the only way. Recognize there are many different jobs to do in the Body; different jobs require different approaches to proper protection. Ask God to cause you to be clearheaded when it comes to training members of His Body in matters of spiritual warfare.

Weaponry

At the beginning of the game, number 43, my nephew, Josh trotted out to the field and took up his position as defensive end. Several plays later, after an interception, he and the rest of the defensive line scrambled off the field and a new batch of players set up to begin a rousing string of offensive plays which led to a touchdown. For you American football fans, I'm proud to say I've learned a thing or two recently about your game. There are two lines within each team, one that advances and one that defends.

I don't know much about military strategy, but I do see the need for offensive and defensive lines in the Body of Christ. I've seen what happens when players stay on the field too long; they cramp and are prone to injury.

I've spent a lot of time in this chapter with my defensive team on the field. I've written of the need for protection, what to protect, and how to protect. Now it's time for a team change. We're 4th and goal and I feel a touchdown coming on. Let's bring on some offense in the form of weapons that are mighty through Christ.

1. The Word

Let's start with the Word, an obvious choice. Having some kind of Bible to bring to Church and study from is a first step toward learning to use this weapon. I know there are purists who like holding a physical Bible of a particular translation, but I'm not one of them. I like a physical Bible, but I prefer to use it mostly at home.

There are so many types of Bibles to choose from these days that there's one suitable for handling just about any adversary at any time. There are electronic Bibles, Bible apps, Bibles on CD, the Bible for Kindle, MP3 Bible files, even One Year Bibles. I think the only one I haven't tried is the slightly older electronic Bible; I just didn't have the money at the time to invest in one.

Think about swords as you consider the plethora of Bibles available. There are long swords, parrying swords, short swords, ceremonial ones, and even little knives. The important thing is that a Bible is chosen through stages of development that will fit the hand and giftings of the one using it. I'm glad a pastor I had several years ago encouraged me to get into the Word through an easy to listen to translation I could play on my MP3 player. I still use those files years later.

Once a child has possession of the Word in some form, learning to use it consistently takes training. Ask to see the Bibles of your children. Are they marked up, highlighted and notated? Unless you're in an exceptionally Word-grounded church, most of them won't be. Get in there and help them change that.

Believe it or not, highlighting, underlining, and writing notes (electronic or otherwise) are skills that need to be taught. Teach children how to do some of these "common sense" things. Go old school to help them learn the Books of the Bible so they can feel comfortable and confident with this remarkable weapon in their hands.

Share your Bible(s) with your children. Let them see what a well broken in Bible looks like. Yes, it is possible to do this electronically too. Tell stories about you and your Bible. Share how you've used it to overcome various weaknesses, problems, and obstacles. They will dig this as much if not more than a recycled Bible lesson!

If you're serious about raising up spiritual children, you have no doubt tried to get children to memorize Scripture as a good discipline. But perhaps you have discovered if they don't learn how to use it, it will most likely be a temporary trick to earn a prize. I myself earned a lot of prizes this way. Next time you see one of your children, ask them to tell you a verse memorized a few months ago. If they haven't had a use for it, they most likely can't recall it.

We teach children the Word is a light to their feet but getting them to understand they are able to use the Word as a weapon against darkness is something we have skipped over for a very long time. This is one reason why learning to pray Scripture is a no brainer. The Word in the heart and hands of a prayer warrior is at home doing what it was designed to do. Advance. Pierce. Slice and dice.

For inspiration, take a look at how other religious groups train their children to use physical weapons. We aren't interested in this except to give a picture of what children are capable of spiritually.

The Church is sitting on an untapped arsenal of glory and power. Glory to God and power over the enemy.

2. Blood of the Lamb + Our Testimony

Revelation 12 says the dragon, the Devil, is cast out of the heavenlies through the blood of the Lamb and the word of the testimony of the saints. Jesus, the Lamb of God, shed His innocent blood for all of mankind to bring glory to God. His blood is powerful and when coupled with our testimony can move and shake the heavenlies.

From this particular description, it appears the word of our testimony, the testimony of the Body, coupled with the blood of the Lamb is what will empower the archangel, Michael and his angels to overcome the dragon and his angels. That is a pretty powerful thought to marinate in. Will my testimony be a life lived to bring God glory or will it be a death that brings Him glory? Either way, as long as God receives glory and the Devil is defeated, I'll be thrilled.

In some regions of the world Christians are already giving their lives as a witness to the power of the blood of the Lamb. Christians living in closed nations have experienced persecution for the last several decades, and in recent years, persecution has increased. Sometimes, perhaps because we are not experiencing intense persecution in Western countries, we are guilty of thinking, "persecution is coming." The truth is, intense persecution of Christians is here on the earth and it has been for quite some time.

Would I be willing to give my life as a testimony? Would you? Would your children? Check out stories from such places as www.persecution.com to see what is currently going on in the world around you. Knowing what others are going through not only helps us pray for God's glory in those situations, but also gives us an opportunity for a little soul-searching.

3. Children's Praise

Are you mentally going through what you know about the power of children's praise? I'm thinking of Psalm 8:2. When children praise, God's enemies are silenced. Great minds think alike, eh?

In a meeting where children praised and worshipped all out, they got lost in it and began a kind of warfare praising. As I stood there watching the scene in front of me, a thought sideswiped me. I know it's a stretch, but you might find it interesting food for thought.

What if the Church released children to praise and worship in such a way that the enemies of God were silenced and their communication system fried? What if as children praised God regularly the entire network of evil spirits was left in utter chaos? You're right, it wouldn't be long until these spirits would organize an offensive attack targeting children and it wouldn't be the first time. Think of the millions of unborn children aborted in America alone over the past forty years. They were silenced before they could silence with praise.

What if, instead of allowing children who praise to walk around with targets on their back, more seasoned warriors laid down cover fire by way of intercession for them? I can't help but wonder if a part of God's plan doesn't include children leading in worship while elders cover them with prayer.

Children worshipping, adults covering in prayer, and Michael and his angels doing battle. This sounds a lot like an incredible mixture of offensive and defensive teams working in tandem for God's ultimate glory.

Some day God's enemies will be silenced for good, but until then, He gets glory from the silence brought on by children's praise. Our part is to support them along the way however possible.

Clearheaded and protected, that's who we are as saints. Covered in faith, love and the confidence of salvation, coordinating offensive and defensive strategies for God's glory. That's who we are as a Body.

> *"There are different kinds of spiritual gifts, but the same Spirit is the source of them all. There are different kinds of service, but we serve the same Lord. God works in different ways, but it is the same God who does the work in all of us...The human body has many parts, but the many parts make up one whole body. So it is with the body of Christ...All of you together are Christ's body, and each of you is a part of it"* (1 Corinthians 12:4-6, 12, 27).

QUESTIONS

1. What five areas need protection?

    a. _____

    b. _____

    c. _____

    d. _____

    e. _____

2. How is a "One size fits all" mentality counter productive when it comes to wearing spiritual armor?

3. There is defensive armor and offensive weapons. In your opinion, what might happen if someone tries to use one without the other?

4. What are the three offensive weapons discussed in this chapter? How are your children being trained to use them?

FURTHER READING

1. *www.kidspray.org.au*, Jane Mackie
    Jane, a pioneer in kids prayer ministry and spiritual development, has many good bits of advice and concepts to pass along.

2. *The Armor of God* by David Walters
    If you are communicating a very basic overview, this small kid-friendly book will be a help.

3. ***Prayer Giftings*** CD/DVD by Thetus Tenney

   Thetus Tenney captures the essence of how something she calls "prayer giftings" compliment our personalities. Available from www.focusedlight.net.

ABOUT THE AUTHOR

Angie Clark has written articles for magazines since the big-haired 80's, and for websites practically since Al Gore "invented the Internet." Through all her travels and time spent abroad, one thing has remained constant; she is passionate about Jesus and is called to cast seed for such passion in others. Angie lives wherever the Holy Spirit sends her. She doesn't have a cat or dog, but enjoys spending time with family and friends, which is immensely more entertaining.

Made in the USA
Charleston, SC
15 September 2013